Christmas Programs
for Children

Poems, Plays and Programs
for a Joyful Celebration

compiled by

Pat Fittro

TM
STANDARD PUBLISHING
Cincinnati, Ohio

Permission is granted to reproduce these programs for ministry
purposes only—not for resale.

Standard Publishing, Cincinnati, Ohio
A division of Standex International Corporation
© 2000 by Standard Publishing

ISBN 0-7847-1166-6

CONTENTS

WELCOME
Mary Ann Green

I would like to welcome you here
To tell you the story so dear
As we do our part to spread good
  cheer.
We're so glad that each of you is
  here.

SMALL
Mary Ann Green

I'm small, that's true.
But I can say
Merry Christmas
To all of you.

THANKS FOR JESUS
Margaret Primrose

Thanks for baby Jesus
  And for His bed of hay.
Thanks because He loves me
  And hears me when I pray.

GENTLE JESUS
Mary Ann Green

To gentle Jesus I humbly bow
All my heart I shall give Him
  now.

CHRISTMAS JOY
Mary Ann Green

Of all the joy Christmastime
  brings
The best is that Jesus is King.

CELEBRATE
Dolores Steger

Some celebrate the holiday
  With fellowship and mirth;
I celebrate the Miracle
  That God once sent to earth.

NO DANGER
Mary Ann Green

(Small boy dressed as a shepherd.)

I saw the babe in a manger
And cried, "Won't he be in
  danger?"

The animals stood all around,
And the shepherds knelt on the
  ground.

His mother smiled at me
And my heart leaped with glee.

Then I knew He was God's Son,
The long-promised Holy One.

FOR ETERNITY
Dolores Steger

It's a star they're following,
As the wise men come to bring
Presents for a newborn King.
As the gifts they then bestow
By the Child, bowing low,
In their wisdom thus they know
Here's a Babe who's meant to be
Ruler and, by God's decree,
Savior for eternity.

IF YOU'D ASK ME
Dolores Steger

If you'd ask me what Christmas is
    all about,
Here's what I'd say, and I'd stand
    up and shout;
It's all about Jesus, the birth of a
    king,
And peace, love and hope is what
    He's offering.

BEST WAY TO CELEBRATE
Cora M. Owen

The best way to celebrate,
  On this bright day of days;
To make sure that Jesus has
  The best of all birthdays.

The best way to celebrate,
  Is being sure to give,
Not just at Christmastime,
  But all the days you live.

I LIKE CHRISTMAS
Margaret Primrose

I like candles,
  I like bells
And the Christmas stories
  My teacher tells.

What's more important
  Than shiny new toys?
The love of Jesus
  For girls and boys.

UNTO HIS OWN
Cora M. Owen

Jesus came unto His own.
  His own received Him not.
They rejected who He was.
  They knew not what He
    brought.

He gave up Heaven's glory,
  To be born among men.
He came to be the Savior.
  They did not know Him then.

Jesus still is reaching out,
  Seeking for all lost souls,
Seeking for acceptance here.
  Saving and making whole.

LOVE, A CHRISTMAS GIFT
Lillian Robbins

Three little words, God loves you,
　Is what I want to say.
It means more than all the pre-
　　sents
　You get on Christmas Day.

A vase may get broken,
　A puzzle can fall apart,
Sweaters and shirts may not fit,
　But love is in the heart.

Love can't be taken away at all.
　You won't outgrow the need.
Love fits your inner soul
　Wherever your life may lead.

So on this Christmas, my greatest
　　wish,
　That joy may grow and grow.
Through all the days that you
　　shall live,
　God loves you, you must know.
Have a happy Christmas!

THE GOOD NEWS
Margaret Primrose

My grandma sent a Christmas
　　card
　And addressed it just to me.
On the back of it she wrote a note,
　"Put this on the Christmas tree."

I think there's a check and good
　　news inside
　About something that I'm to
　　buy.
I can hardly wait to see for sure,
　But I guess I'll have to try.

I also know of some other Good
　　News
　That I don't have to wait to read,
So let me open a wonderful Book
　And share what's Good News
　　indeed.

*(Read Luke 2:9-11 and 2 Corinthians
9:15.)*

HERE THEY COME
Dolores Steger

Here come the angels,
　They've come to proclaim
A King has been born,
　As the Lord He will reign.

Here come the shepherds,
　They've come to behold
A baby, named Jesus,
　As the angel has told.

Here come the wise men,
　They've come to adore
An infant, a ruler,
　Whom they bow before.

Here come the people,
　They've come to believe
This Savior is theirs,
　As His grace they receive.

THE SHEPHERD BOY'S STORY
Margaret Primrose

My father had watered our little
  flock
  And counted each woolly sheep.
He was pouring oil on a lamb's
  wounded leg
  While I was falling asleep.

I woke all at once when an angel
  appeared,
  And the camp was encircled in
  light.
Was it just a dream, or could I
  believe
  That a miracle was happening
  that night?

How I wished for a tent in which
  to hide,
  For there was no place to go.
"Fear not," I heard the angel say
  As I shook from head to toe.

"I bring you good news," the
  angel said,
  And announced our Savior's
  birth.
Then a throng of angels praised
  the Lord
  For sending Him to earth.

We found the Babe in Bethlehem
  In a lowly cattle stall,
But He truly is the Son of God
  Who came to save us all.

WHAT DO I SEE THERE?
Dolores Steger

What do I see there?
  A baby could it be?
I'll look a little closer;
  It's Jesus who I see;

In His hands I see strength;
  In His eyes I see grace,
And love's what I see
  In the smile on His face;

What did I see there?
  I'll tell you if I can;
I saw the Lord, the Savior,
  The Redeemer of man.

SEEKING GIFTS...

OR SEEKING THE GIVER

THE BEST GIFT
Lillian Robbins

Christmas is Jesus' birthday,
  But no balloons are there.
No pretty little packages
  Stacked upon a chair.

Jesus is the present
  Sent to all the world.
He's the greatest gift of all
  For every boy and girl.

I May Be Small

C. R. Scheidies

(For one or more children)

1: *(Hold up picture of manger.)*
I may be small, but not too small,
To know Jesus came in a manger
stall.

2: *(Mimic rocking baby.)*
He came as a baby so tiny and
new.
Came as a baby for me and for
you. *(Point, me to you.)*

3: Jesus came as a baby, God's
only Son,
To show His great love for everyone. *(Make circle with arms, as
though including whole world.)*

All: Yes, we may be small, but not
too small *(Shake heads.)*
To say, "Thank You Jesus, for loving us one and all." *(Raise
hands. All recite* John 3:16.*)*

"Joy to the World" *(first and last
stanzas. Optional: "Away in a
Manger")*

C Is for . . .

Mary Ann Green

*(Eleven small children with large
letter cards.)*

C is for the Christ child
H is for His Home in my heart.
R is to Remember His lowly birth.
I is as an Infant He came.
S is for our Savior
T it's Time to worship Him.

C is for the Coming King.
H is for the Happiness He brings.
I is that He lives In my heart.
L is for the Love He shares.
D is for His Daily care.

The First Christmas

Alyce Pickett

Child 1
I couldn't be on the hillside
To hear the angels sing;
I couldn't go with the shepherds
To find the Christ child king,

Child 2
I couldn't follow the bright star
That showed magi the way
To Bethlehem's lowly stable
Where little Jesus lay.

Both
But we can praise Him, so can
you, *(Indicate audience.)*
The Babe with smile bright,
Who came to be our Savior
On that first Christmas night.

WHAT IS CHRISTMAS DAY MADE OF?
Helen Kitchell Evans

Child 1: What is Christmas Day made of, made of?
           What is Christmas Day made of?
Child 2: It's made of lovely Christmas trees,
Child 3: It's made of people who want to please,
Child 4: It's made of candles that are bright,
Child 5: It's made of a star on Christmas night;
Child 6: It's made of love because a child came,
Child 7: It's Jesus, of course, we all know His name.
All: That's what Christmas Day is made of.
           That's what Christmas Day is made of, made of!

BELLS, A STAR AND A MANGER
Margaret Primrose

Child 1: Silver bells, silver bells, sing your song.
           Make it clear and loud and long.
           Tell the world of a Savior dear
           Who stays beside us all through the year.
Child 2: Twinkle, twinkle star on high,
           Gleaming in the eastern sky,
           Be like the star that led the way
           To where the baby Jesus lay.
Child 3: Manger, manger in a wee stall,
           You held the greatest Gift of all—
           Not myrrh, nor frankincense, nor gold,
           But One whose love will never grow cold.
Child 4: A star, some bells and a manger
           Are only lifeless things;
           But they help us to remember
           The joy that Christmas brings.

           I'm glad that when I see them,
           I think of God's great love
           And thank Him for the baby
           He sent us from above.

Christmas Manger Service

Mary Rose Pearson

Characters:
Narrator
Mary
Shepherd
Angel
Wise man
Six modern-day children

Costumes: Bible characters should be in costume.

Props: A clock and some dollar bills

Scene: A manger with a doll, a stool for Mary

Stage Directions: Speakers enter, say the lines and then go to their places in the tableau. Mary sits on the stool. The shepherd kneels at the manger and the wise man stands on the side. Others follow the directions given.

Narrator:	Within a manger filled with hay There lay the Son of God one day; And gifts were brought by those who came That they might praise His worthy name.
Mary:	His mother gave Him all her care And offered up a humble prayer. *(Sits.)*
Shepherd:	The shepherds brought a gift of praise To honor Him that day of days. *(Kneels.)*
Wise man:	The wise men watched the star above And later brought their gifts of love. *(Stands on one side.)*
Narrator:	A gift for Christ we too should bring To honor Him, our Lord and King; But what have we that He would heed? What gifts of ours would He need?

(The six children enter and stand in line, facing the audience.)

First Child:	*(Holding hand over heart.)* I want to give to Him my heart, And in His pathway I will start. *(Looks up.)* Lord Jesus, I believe in You; Forgive my sins; help me to be true.
Second Child:	*(Holding out both hands.)* I'd like to give to Him my hands, To work for Him in far-off lands. But now I'll serve Him here each day, That those unsaved might find the way.
Third Child:	*(Pointing toward feet.)* I'd like to give my feet to Him, I'll walk His path, though it be dim. That I may lead those far astray To His bright land of fairest day.
Fourth Child:	*(Pointing to mouth.)* My gift is small—my tongue I bring, That I may never cease to sing His praises ev'rywhere I go; My love to Him I want to show.
Fifth Child:	*(Holding a clock.)* I have a gift of time to give That ev'ry moment I may live, For Him who gave His life for me Upon the cross of Calvary.
Sixth Child:	*(Holding some money.)* I bring my money to Him now; It's His—not mine—I truly vow, So many more may come to know Of Jesus Christ, who loves us so.

(All children kneel in a semicircle, facing the manger.)

All:	Oh, Lord we bow before Your throne; For all we have is now Your own. Please take us; use us in Your way; Accept our gifts to You today.

MARCH OF THE CHRISTMAS SYMBOLS

Dorothy M. Page

Characters:

Angel	Card
Carol	Bell
Wreath	Crèche
Candle	Drummer Boy
Tree	

This program requires nine characters. The characters may carry placards picturing the symbols they represent, or they may be dressed as the symbols they represent, or they may carry the object they represent. They march on stage, single file, to the drum and music of "Little Drummer Boy."

Angel: I am a Christmas angel.
I sang at the holy birth
In the choir of heavenly voices
Proclaiming peace on earth.

Carol: I am a Christmas carol.
Each year at Christmastime
My music and words bring joy
In special Christmas rhyme.

Wreath: I am a Christmas wreath.
My leaves and berries glow.
I bring a wealth of color
With my big, red satin bow.

Candle: I am a Christmas candle.
My light will guide the way
For weary pilgrims searching for
A place where they may pray.

Tree: I am a little Christmas tree
All bright with tinsel trim.
Children find their Christmas gifts
Beneath each spreading limb.

Card: I am a special Christmas card.
My message comes to bring
News of the holy birth
Of Jesus Christ our king.

Bell: I am a silver Christmas bell.
               My joyous ringing comes to say
               That long ago the Holy Child
               Was born on Christmas Day.

Crèche: I am a Christmas crèche,
               And represent the scene
               Of the humble stable birthplace
               By prophecy foreseen.

When recitations are completed, the group marches out to the "Little Drummer Boy."

Why Do We Celebrate Christmas?

Dorothy M. Page

Characters:
Angel Speaker, only speaking part
Group of present-day Christmas shoppers
Woman pushing baby carriage
Group of travelers in biblical costumes
Mary, Joseph, baby or doll
Two or three shepherds
Two or three angels

This program begins with closed curtain onstage. To a loud blast of secular music ("Jingle Bell Rock" or other nonreligious music) the group of present-day shoppers loaded with Christmas packages, hurries across the stage in front of the closed curtain. Last to cross is the woman pushing a baby carriage. When this woman is about halfway across the stage, the music softens. The Angel Speaker steps out and smiles into the baby carriage. The woman goes on offstage. The music stops.

Angel Speaker:　In the cacophony
　　　　　　　　　Of Christmas December
　　　　　　　　　A baby sleeps—
　　　　　　　　　And I remember . . .

(Angel pauses as though thinking.)

Angel Speaker:　In the press of travelers . . .

(Group of persons in biblical costumes start across in front of the closed curtain, shoving and pushing and talking in angry, loud tones. They pass, and speaker continues.)

Angel Speaker:　In the press of travelers
　　　　　　　　　No room in the inn.
　　　　　　　　　The baby Jesus slept
　　　　　　　　　In a stable bin.

(Curtain opens to reveal a nativity scene with Mary, Joseph and baby. Shepherds enter and kneel around the baby.)

Angel Speaker: Those favored shepherds
Who looked on His face
Never noticed the waste
In that lowly place.

(Angels enter and stand in background. This part may be enhanced by having the angels sing "Joy to the World.")

Angel Speaker: And the heavenly angels
Who sang at His birth
Knew wherever He lay
Was sacred on earth.

(Singing starts with second verse and gradually fades away.)

Angel Speaker: Has earth grown weary
Of the precious story,
Of His holy birth
And hymns of His glory?

How few of the songs
Mention His birth.
Seems all they want
Is commercial worth.

Come, all His people!
Keep Christ the real reason
To celebrate Christmas
This holiday season.

Buddy Bird Speaks

Dixie Phillips

"Buddy Bird Speaks" is a delightful Christmas play that gives a little glimpse into human nature. Grandma Leora is forced to move from her farm to a small apartment because of her ill health. She is not allowed to take her favorite pet parrot, Buddy Bird, with her. Three young girls whom she has befriended decide they each want Buddy Bird. Grandma Leora has a very tough decision to make. Who should get her beloved pet? After much thought Grandma Leora has the wisdom of Solomon. Listen and you will see how "prompt obedience" caused one of these young girls to receive a "prompt blessing"!

Characters:
Grandma Leora, an elderly woman
Lynne, neighbor girl
Melissa, neighbor girl
Morgan, neighbor girl
Buddy Bird, should be a child who has "great" expression with his/her voice. This child will not be seen in the play, but will be heard. He should be hidden behind a curtain and have access to a good microphone so the audience can hear the comments Buddy makes.

Scene 1

Scene 1 begins with Grandma Leora sitting in a rocking chair looking tenderly into a bird cage set on an end table.

Grandma Leora: Oh, Buddy! I sure am going to miss you when I move to town. But you know life is always changing. They won't let me have any pets there! No dogs . . . no cats . . . no gerbils . . . no hamsters . . . no birds. Not even a well-behaved parrot like you, Buddy! I tell you, old age is not for sissies! *(Reaches in cage and scratches top of Buddy's head.)* Now don't you worry, my fine-feathered friend, I'll be sure to find you a good home.

(A knock comes to Grandma Leora's door.)

Grandma Leora: I'm coming. Just hold your horses!

(Grandma opens the door to see her three friends.)

Lynne: It's just us, your very own fan club.
Grandma Leora: Well, it's my little friends from the neighborhood. Now what brings you "three musketeers" to my house?
Melissa: We just heard some awful news. We heard you were going to move away. Is that true?
Grandma Leora: Yes, I'm afraid it is.
Melissa: Well, we'll really miss you. We've brought you some cookies.

(Melissa gives cookie tin to Grandma. Grandma peeks inside.)

Grandma Leora: Mmm-m-m! Shortbread, my favorite.
Morgan: And that's not all. We even brought you some of your favorite French vanilla coffee.

(Morgan holds up a tin of coffee.)

Grandma Leora: Well, it's a good thing I haven't packed "our" favorite coffee cups yet. Come on in and we'll have ourselves a little coffee break. I'll really miss our special times together.

(All three girls and Grandma go over to a table and begin setting it with cups and saucers. Buddy Bird's cage is nearby. At this time the child will squawk Buddy Bird's part into the microphone.)

Buddy Bird: Awwwk! Cup of tea! Cup of tea! Awwwk! One lump or two!
Grandma Leora: Now, Buddy Bird . . . you're showing how smart you are! We're not drinking tea. We're drinking coffee.
Morgan: Is there anything he can't say?
Grandma Leora: He is one smart bird! I surely will miss him!
Lynne: You mean Buddy Bird can't go with you?
Grandma Leora *(sadly):* I'm afraid not! They won't allow pets where I'm moving to.
Melissa: Where will he go?
Grandma Leora: I don't know. I do want to find someone who will be good to him.
Lynne: I'll take him.
Melissa: I'd take extra-good care of him.
Morgan: He can come live with me.
Buddy Bird: Awwwk! Pretty bird! Pretty bird!
Grandma Leora *(snapping fingers):* I know! We'll let Buddy Bird decide

for himself where he wants to live. He can decide for himself.

Melissa: I know Buddy is really smart, but how is he going to tell you who he wants to live with?

Grandma Leora: You each may take Buddy Bird home for two days. Then, you bring him back to me. He will let me know which one of you will take the best care of him.

Lynne: Let's see. That's six days from now. That will be Christmas Day. Wow! One of us will get the neatest Christmas present ever.

Morgan: I get him first.

Melissa: Me second.

Grandma Leora: And Lynne will get him third.

(Grandma places a blanket over Buddy Bird's cage and hands it to Morgan.)

Grandma Leora: Just be sure he has plenty of water and seed. I'll see you girls on Christmas Day.

Scene 2

Scene 2 begins with Grandma Leora humming a familiar Christmas carol as she is baking some Christmas cookies. She is interrupted by a knock at the door.

Grandma Leora: I bet it's the girls and Buddy Bird.

(She opens the door. The three girls are beaming with enthusiasm.)

Melissa: Here's Buddy Bird. We each took really good care of him!

Morgan: Yes, we fed him and watered him every day just like you told us to.

Lynne: And now we just have to wait for Buddy Bird to tell you who he wants to live with.

(Grandma Leora carries Buddy Bird's cage over closer to her rocking chair and sets it on the end table. She removes the blanket.)

Grandma Leora: Good morning, Buddy Bird.

Buddy Bird: Awwwk! Good morning, Buddy Bird.

Grandma Leora: Morgan, come here!

Buddy Bird: Awwwk! Morgan, come here! Just a minute, Mother.

(Morgan places her hands over her mouth and gasps!)

Grandma Leora: Melissa, come here!

Buddy Bird: Awwwwk! Melissa, come here! Not now, Mother. Later. Awwwk!

(Melissa and Morgan stare at Buddy Bird in disbelief and horror.)

Grandma Leora: Lynne, come here!

Buddy Bird: Awwwk! Lynne, come here! Awwwk! Coming, Mother.

(Grandma Leora picks up the cage and places it in Lynne's hands.)

Grandma Leora: Well, Buddy Bird has spoken.

Girls *(in unison):* I'll say.

Grandma Leora: You know there's a Christmas message in what we saw just now.

Girls *(in unison):* What's that?

Grandma Leora: Well, it's this: "Prompt obedience is the best kind of obedience." When God was ready to send Jesus to earth as a baby. Jesus promptly obeyed. He didn't say, "Later, Father," or "Not now, Father," but He promptly obeyed. I'm so glad He did.

Girls *(in unison):* Me too.

Melissa: Well, I've sure learned a lesson today.

Morgan: Me too. Prompt obedience is the best obedience.

Grandma Leora: Well, Lynne, Merry Christmas. I know you will take good care of Buddy Bird.

Lynne: I sure will.

Buddy Bird: Awwwk!!!! Merry Christmas to all.

THE VERY BEST CHRISTMAS GIFT

Jeanne K. Grieser

Characters:
Girl 1, dressed in street clothes
Girl 2, dressed in street clothes
Angel Visitor, dressed in white
Mary, dressed in blue
Joseph, brown robe
Wise men (3), robes
Innkeepers (4), clothes from Jesus' day
Shepherds (2), brown clothes/robes
Angels (4), white robes
Caesar Augustus, military attire from Jesus' day
Herod, kingly attire from Bible times
Roman Guard, military attire from Jesus' day
Choir or Soloist

Props: Stable with star on top, manger, donkey, shepherds' staffs, wise
men gifts, baby doll, blue/white cloth (for Jesus), straw, small wooden
chair, fabric, needle and thread, scroll

Scene 1—The Visitor

Two girls enter talking, from stage left.

Girl 1: What do you want for Christmas?
Girl 2: I want a CD player, but my parents can't afford much since my
dad lost his job. Christmas this year won't be special at all.
Girl 1: Christmas is always special!
Girl 2: Not without presents.
Girl 1: Why don't you come to church with me tonight? Then you'll see
why Christmas is special.
Girl 2: I think I'm busy.
Girl 1: But it's Christmas Eve. Don't you want to hear the Christmas
story?
Girl 2: Will I get presents if I come?
Girl 1: Well, we will get a bag of peanuts and candy.
Girl 2: Oh. I'm not sure.

Angel Visitor *(walks in from stage right and appears behind girls):* Maybe I can help.

Girl 1: Where did you come from?

Girl 2: What will you help with?

Visitor: I heard you talking about presents and Christmas. I had to come down and visit you. Christmas is my favorite time of year!

Girl 2: It's not so special without presents.

Visitor: Sit down and let me tell you about a special present. The story begins a long time ago.

(Girls and Visitor sit down on the center/left stage. Mary enters from right stage, sits on chair and sews.)

Scene 2—The Announcement

As Mary sews, an Angel enters from stage right. Mary looks up in shock and falls to her knees.

Angel: Greetings, Mary. The Lord is with you. Do not be afraid. God has decided to bless you wonderfully! Very soon you will become pregnant and have a baby boy. You will name Him Jesus. He shall be great! He shall be called the Son of the Most High.

Mary: But how can I have a baby? I am a virgin.

Angel: The Holy Spirit shall come upon you and the power of God shall overshadow you. The Holy One to be born will be called the Son of God. Nothing is impossible with God.

Mary: I am the Lord's servant. I will do what He wants me to do.

(Mary and Angel leave.)

Song: "Come, Thou Long-Expected Jesus"

(Enter Caesar Augustus from stage right.)

Caesar Augustus *(reading loudly, proclaiming from scroll):* I, Caesar Augustus, hereby issue a decree that a census shall be taken throughout this nation. Everyone must return to his hometown to register and pay his taxes. *(He leaves.)*

Scene 3—The Birth

Visitor: Joseph had to pay taxes also, and because he was a descendant of David, he had to go to Bethlehem in Judea to register. Mary traveled with Joseph. She was expecting a child. The trip from Nazareth was long and tiring. They traveled seventy miles. Joseph walked and Mary may have walked or ridden on a donkey.

(Enter Mary, maybe on a donkey, and Joseph down center aisle and walk onto center stage.)

Girl 2: Did they stay in a nice hotel?

(Enter four innkeepers. They line up across center stage. Joseph stops by one at a time.)

Joseph: Excuse me, Sir. We've traveled far. Do you have a room we can rent?
Innkeeper 1: I'm sorry. I have no room.
Joseph: Sir, do you have a room we can rent?
Innkeeper 2: I'm sorry. I just rented my last room.
Joseph: Sir, we are tired. We need a place to stay. Do you have a room where we can stay?
Innkeeper 3: No. My rooms are full.
Joseph: Sir, Mary is expecting a child. Our travel has worn her out. Do you have room for us?
Innkeeper 4: I'm sorry, but my inn is full.
Joseph: We'll even take a small room.
Innkeeper 4 *(jokingly):* Everything is full in this town except the stables.

(Mary and Joseph exchange looks. Mary nods.)

Joseph: Do you have a stable we could stay in? We'd be most grateful.
Innkeeper 4: Sure, but I have some animals inside.
Joseph: It doesn't matter. *(Shake hands.)* Thank you so much.

(Mary and Joseph walk to stable. Innkeepers exit.)

Girl 2: Mary didn't have her baby in that dirty stable, did she?

(As Visitor talks, Mary picks up baby, wraps him in a cloth. Joseph takes clean straw and places it in the manger. Mary lays baby in manger.)

Visitor: While they were in the Bethlehem stable, the time came for the baby to be born. She gave birth to her firstborn, a Son. She wrapped Him in strips of cloth and placed Him in a manger.

Song: "Joyful, Joyful, We Adore Thee"

Visitor: Nearby in a field, shepherds were watching their flocks of sheep.

Scene 4—Bearing Gifts

Shepherds enter down center aisle at end of song. They recline and/or sit on steps of center stage.

Shepherd 1: I wonder where Ben is? He should have been back by now.
Shepherd 2: Bethlehem is full of people. When Caesar Augustus says to pay taxes, we pay taxes.
Shepherd 1: Yes, you're right. *(Pause briefly.)* The land seems unusually quiet tonight. The air is crisp and clear.
Shepherd 2: Yes, are we expecting something, like . . . a storm?

(Angels enter from stage right. Shepherds are afraid.)

Angel: Don't be afraid! I bring you good news of great joy for all people. Today in the town of David a Savior has been born. He is Christ! He is the Lord! This will be a sign for you: you will find a baby wrapped in cloths and lying in a manger.

Song *(Angels sing):* "Gloria" *(© 1979 by Les Presses de Taizé in France.)*

Shepherd 1: Let's go to Bethlehem now!
Shepherd 2: Let's see this wonderful thing that has happened.

(Shepherds and Angels go to the stable.)

Girl 2: Why did God want some smelly shepherds to know about Jesus' birth first?
Visitor: Baby Jesus came for everyone.
Girl 2 *(points to self):* For me?

(Visitor smiles and nods.)

Song: "Go, Tell It on the Mountain"

Visitor: After Jesus was born, magi or wise men from the east saw a bright star in the sky and they followed it a long way to Jerusalem. They went to King Herod's palace for more information.

(Enter three wise men down center aisle at end of song. Enter King Herod and Roman Guard from stage right. Stand near center of stage.)

Wise man 1: Kind Sir, where is the One born King of the Jews?
Herod: What king? I'm the king. *(To Roman Guard.)* Go and call the chief priests and teachers of the law together. Ask them where this Christ was to be born. *(Guard leaves.)* You say you're from the east?
Wise man 1: Yes. We study the stars. One evening a brilliant star came into view.
Wise man 2: We knew then that the Messiah had been born. God has given us a sign.
Wise man 3: We followed the star and have come to worship the King.

(Enter Roman Guard.)

Herod: So what have you found?
Roman Guard: The prophet Micah predicted that the Christ child would be born in Bethlehem. He will be a governor to rule the people of Israel.
Herod: Very well then. *(To Wise men.)* Make a careful search for this child. As soon as you find Him, report back to me. I want to worship Him too.
Wise man 1: We shall tell you when we return.

(Wise men start to go to the stable. Herod and Roman Guard leave.)

Wise man 2 *(points):* Look! There's the place.

(Walk to stable. Stand in front of the manger.)

Song: "Joy to the World!"

Wise man 1: I have brought gold for the King. *(Lays down gift.)*
Wise man 2: I have brought Him frankincense. *(Lays down gift.)*
Wise man 3: I have brought myrrh for the Christ child. *(Lays down gift.)*
Mary: I am overwhelmed. My heart is full of joy.
Shepherd 1: We are poor shepherds. We have no gifts to offer, except our love for the Messiah.

Shepherd 2: Praise be to God!

Mary: That is all God asks. Peace to all of you.

Joseph: You have come to worship God's Son. He is no ordinary baby. This baby is the newborn King.

Wise man 1: We should quickly leave and tell Herod where Jesus is.

Wise man 2: No. I have been warned in a dream not to go back to Herod. He wants to hurt the King. We shall travel home by a different route.

(Girls and Visitor stand.)

Girl 2: That's an amazing story. I felt like I was in Bethlehem watching it all happen.

Girl 1: I've heard the story many times, but it was extra special hearing you tell it.

Visitor: Children all over the world will hear this special story tonight and the world will never forget His birthday and His Gift. Every Christmas the heavens rejoice with the world.

Girl 2: What gift? What about the presents?

Girl 1: God's present to us is Jesus.

Girl 2: But what present can I give to Jesus?

Visitor: All Jesus wants from you is your heart—your love.

Girl 2: Wow! Jesus is the best present ever! Christmas is special because it's all about Jesus and not about CD players.

Song *(by Girl 2 and/or 1):* "Christmas Isn't Christmas" *(Written by Jimmy and Carol Owens, can be found in "All the Best Songs for Kids.")*

Girl 2 *(bows head and folds hands):* Let's pray. Thank You, Jesus, for coming to earth for me! I will never forget Your birthday because I love You. Amen.

(Visitor quickly exits during prayer.)

Girl 1 *(looking around):* Where did she go?

Girl 2: She was beautiful. Do you think she was an angel?

Girl 1: Maybe. *(Looks toward the sky.)*

Girl 2: What time did you say your church service will start?

Girl 1: Seven o'clock.

Girl 2: I'll see you there.

(Girls leave.)

THE NATIVITY

Julia Whitehair

Characters:

Narrator	Shepherd 2
Child 1	Shepherd 3
Child 2	Angel
Child 3	Wise man 1
Mary	Wise man 2
Joseph	Wise man 3
Innkeeper	Ballerina
Shepherd 1	

Other angels, shepherds and wise men are optional and can participate in group lines. Smaller children can be used as animals.

Props: Figurines of nativity characters and ballerina doll

Scene 2 was adapted from "Once Upon a Christmas" written by Catherine Smith. The play is written for elementary through high school age students. The manger scene may be set up in front of the stage or to one side. The nativity characters appear as figurines. They take their places on stage and don't move, but remain statue-like until Scene 2. Lighting can be used to emphasize the movement from the children to the nativity characters. Use the names of the children where the blanks are.

Scene 1

Living room scene. Lights on piano. Children holding the pieces of a manger scene enter from the back of the church.

Narrator: It's December at the Smith family home. All the little Smiths are helping decorate the house for the holidays. Child 1 and Child 2 are putting the manger scene on a table.

(Child 1 unwraps figurines and sets them on a table, while Child 2 watches.)

Child 1: Mom said to be careful with the manger scene, ____, so I'd better put it up. You might drop it.

Child 2: Can I watch, ____?

Child 1: I guess so. Just don't touch anything!

Child 3: Let's hurry so we can get to the Christmas tree!

Child 2 *(picking up Mary)*: Who's this, ____? She's pretty.

Child 1 *(snatching figure away)*: I said don't touch. This is Mary. She's the first figurine Mom ever had.

Child 2: Why?

Child 1: Mom's Sunday school teacher gave Mary to Mom for Christmas. It was the Christmas after I was born. Mom said it was special because she and Mary were both new moms at Christmas.

(Lights on stage. Mary enters, holding Jesus, hums to Him. Cast sings "Silent Night! Holy Night!" Mary takes place on stage, lays Jesus in manger, and freezes as lights go back to piano.)

Song: "Silent Night! Holy Night!" *(Cast sings.)*

Child 3: Can we go to the tree now?

Child 2: Who was the next figurine Mom got for the manger scene?

Child 1 *(holds up Joseph)*: This guy, Joseph. He's Mary's husband.

Child 2: What does he do?

Child 1 *(places Joseph in nativity)*: He stands here next to Mary. Daddy gave Joseph to Mom for their fifth anniversary. He said he wanted to be as good a husband as Joseph was.

(Lights on stage. Joseph enters. Joseph has a staff. Joseph takes place and freezes as Cast sings.)

Song: "O Come, All Ye Faithful" *(Cast sings.)*

Child 3: Time to go to the tree, please?

Child 2: Where was Jesus born? Was he born in a hospital like I was?

Child 1: No, silly. He was born in Bethlehem, in a barn. There were so many people in Bethlehem to pay their taxes that there was no room for Mary and Joseph at the inn.

Child 2: Who gave Mommy this person? *(Picks up the innkeeper figurine.)*

Child 1: Mom bought the innkeeper that year we had to stay in the hotel over Christmas.

Child 2: I don't remember that. Why were we there?

Child 1: Our house wasn't built yet, so we had to stay in a hotel. Mommy bought the innkeeper to remind us that Jesus spent Christmas in an inn, too.

(Lights on stage. Innkeeper enters saying, "No room, I tell you! No room!")

Song: "Away in a Manger" (*Cast sings, light to piano.*)

Child 2: Who are these men?
Child 1: They're shepherds. See the sheep?
Child 2: Why were they there?
Child 1: They were visiting Jesus after He was born. Mom's friend gave her these shepherds for Christmas, because the friend visited Mom when she was in the hospital after you and I were born.
Child 3: Can we please see the tree now?

(*Lights on stage. Shepherds enter with sheep. All take their places in the manger scene and freeze.*)

Song: "The First Noel" (*Cast sings, light to piano.*)

Child 2: How did the shepherds know where Jesus was? Did they send a birth announcement?
Child 1: No, ____. Angels told them. See the angel here? (*Holds up angel figurine.*)
Child 2: Where did we get the angel?
Child 1: Mommy got it one Christmas from the choir she directs at church.

(*Lights on stage. Angel(s) enter. Angels take their places as cast sings. They freeze. Lights to piano.*)

Song: "Hark! the Herald Angels Sing" (*Cast sings.*)

Child 1: Do you know who these guys are?
Child 2: They look like kings.
Child 1: Close! They're wise men.
Child 2: Oh, yeah! I heard about them in Sunday school. They visited Jesus too.
Child 1: Uh-huh. They followed a star to find Jesus.
Child 2: I remember these! Daddy got them last year from his Sunday school class. They said he was a "wise man."
Child 3 (*picks up wise man*): I bet they didn't have to wait so long to see their Christmas tree.

(*Lights on stage. Wise men enter, take their places and freeze. Lights to piano.*)

Song: "We Three Kings" (*Cast sings.*)

Child 2: What figurine did we get this year?

Child 1 *(sadly):* Most of these figurines have been gifts. We'll have to see if we get a new one this year.

Child 2 *(hopefully):* We could go look.

Child 3: Hooray! Now we can see the tree.

Child 1 and 2: Wow! Let's go, etc.

(Children start to run away. Child 3 comes back and places doll in manger scene.)

Child 3: Here, Dolly. Now you can learn about baby Jesus too.

(Ballerina twirls to stage. Lights to stage.)

Scene 2—The Nativity

Shepherd 1 *(stretching and shaking out robe):* Here we are again. I was beginning to get itchy. Frankly, I feel cramped in that box with no light, no air, no nothing.

Shepherd 2: Oh, I never complain. I'm always wrapped in that soft tissue paper.

Shepherd 1: I like the tissue paper all right, providing they don't get it around my neck too tightly. *(Rubs neck.)*

Shepherd 2 and 3 *(nodding heads):* You have a point there.

Shepherd 2 *(rubs neck):* I wouldn't want to be choked either.

Shepherd 3: Last year the lambs nuzzled my robe, but no matter.

Shepherd 1: I feel happy being here.

Shepherd 3: Angels, are you here again this year?

Angels: We're here, good shepherd!

Shepherd 3: Angels, can you see all of us?

Angel 1: Oh, yes, shepherd. My position is very good this year.

Shepherd 1: Angel, will you tell me where we stand?

Shepherd 2: Yes, that little girl has me placed so that all I can see is Joseph's back.

Angel 1: Shepherd, dear, it is quite clear
That we're all here again this year. *(Shepherds nod in agreement.)*
The three wise men in raiment fine *(Wise men bow.)*
Stand holding gifts for the child divine.
Our sweet-faced, loving Mary *(Mary picks up baby.)*
So adoringly she tends her baby. *(Rock baby.)*
And Joseph, strong, so full of pride *(Joseph stands up straight, proud.)*
Is watching closely at her side.

Shepherd 3: That's wonderful, Angel. (*Angel curtsies or bows.*)

Shepherd 2: All accounted for.

Shepherd 1: And no broken pieces.

Innkeeper (*confused*): Oh, Angel, who is this new figurine in front of me?

Angel 1 (*confused*): Why, I don't know, good Innkeeper. Why don't you ask her?

Innkeeper (*taps doll*): Excuse me, good lady, but who are you?

Doll (*twirls*): I am a ballerina.

Wise man 1: A ballerina?

Wise man 2: What's a ballerina?

Wise man 3: Where are they in the manger scene?

Doll (*confused*): Manger scene? What manger scene?

Shepherd 1 (*can't believe his/her ears*): You mean you don't know about the manger scene?

Shepherd 2: The baby Jesus?

Shepherd 3: The good news?

Doll: I don't know what story you're talking about.

Joseph: Oh, dear. You are in the middle of the manger scene.

Mary: What can we do?

Doll (*points to side*): What if I sit over there and listen? Maybe I can learn about this manger scene.

Joseph (*relieved*): Oh, that would be much better.

Doll: All right! (*Twirls and dances to the side of the manger scene and sits down.*)

Angel 1: There. Now we're all right.

Shepherd 3: You know, Angel, your voice is uncommonly sweet this year.

Wise man 1: Yes, Angels, you bring a heavenly peace. (*Sighs.*)

Angels: Thank you, Wise man.

Wise man 1: Angel, you say we three wise men are dressed in raiment fine, but would you look at my beard? The little girl nearly dropped me in her excitement to get to the tree.

Wise man 2: She is always in such a hurry to get to the tree.

Wise man 3: I noticed that too.

Wise man 1: The Christmas tree must be a rare variety among trees.

Wise man 2: They value it highly.

Wise man 3: Angel, will you please check my robe? The girl pulled it when she took me out of the box, and I fear the folds may be crooked.

Joseph: Great Wise men, you are always so concerned about your beards and robes. As for me, I would be happy if just once I could see Mary's face.

Shepherd 1: It must be goodness itself.

Shepherd 2: The tilt of her head as she watches the baby makes me think that her eyes shower soft gentleness.

Wise man 1: It is true.

Wise man 2: Mary's face must be beautiful.

Wise man 3: I would give much to see it, but I take joy in watching the baby Jesus.

Shepherd 3: Wise men, do you know why they take us out of the box for a little time each year?

Shepherd 1 and 2: Yes, please tell us.

Wise man 1: Shepherd, we thought about it a lot.

Wise man 2: Finally, we came to a conclusion.

Wise man 3: The baby Jesus is the explanation.

Innkeeper: What makes you think so?

Mary: Oh, learned Wise man, do you truly believe the baby is the reason?

Joseph: He's such a small little thing.

All Wise men: Yes, we do.

Ballerina (*twirls and dances to stage*): Oh, now I understand! The baby is the reason for Christmas!

Wise man 1: The angel told us that when they take us from the box, they arrange us so that we all face the baby.

Angel 1: Even our bodies incline to Him.

Mary: Oh, Wise men, this gives me such happiness
I can feel the real Child's godliness.
He seems to glow with radiant light.
I feel the flow of His heavenly might.

(All characters come to the front. Cast sings a Christmas carol. At the conclusion of the song, all turn to audience and bow.)

It's a Small World at Christmastime

Lucy Robbins and Dixie Phillips

This little skit can be as simple or as elaborate as you would like it to be. If you can find native costumes, that's great. If not, don't be discouraged, a simple sash with the name of the country written across it will suffice. Remember, children have a way of "stealing the show" without elaborate scenery. A table should be placed stage right. As the children enter with their props in hand, they recite their lines, then place their props on the empty table. Also, an empty manger bed should be centrally located so after the Unity Child speaks he could place the dolly in the manger.

Characters:

Welcome Child	Guatemalan Child
Narrator 1	Haitian Child
Narrator 2	American Child
Narrator 3	Unity Child
Indian Child	Deaf Child
Japanese Child	Lame Child
Irish Child	Blind Child
German Child	Final Child
Korean Child	

Welcome Child: It's my job to stand and say, *(Louder.)*
"Welcome to our Christmas play."
So, come on in *(Motions.)* and grab a seat,
You are in for a really big treat!

Narrator 1: Christians celebrate Christmas in all lands,
Some bow their heads. Some lift their hands.
In this play tonight, you will see,
Just how different each one can be.
Though we're different, we're kind of the same.
Because we worship and praise His holy name.

Indian Child *(enters carrying clay pot with candle):*
In southern India, where I come from,
This is how the Christmas celebration is done.
We fill little clay lamps with oil and a wick.
It really is a pretty neat trick. *(Winks.)*
We put them around the house both high and low.

So that each one who passes by will know—
This is how we let our light shine,
For Baby Jesus at Christmastime.

Japanese Child *(enters carrying a small cake):*
Christmas is the time of year,
When to Jesus we draw near.
In Japan, we take this time to say,
We want to serve others in a Christian way.

Irish Child *(enters carrying a lit candle):*
On Christmas Eve, in Ireland,
Our tradition is so grand!
A candle is lit for all to know,
God's kindness, we will gladly show.
If anyone has a need, he can come on in,
We'll point the weary soul to Him!

German Child *(enters carrying Christmas tree lights):*
Germany has a great tradition, you see.
We put lights on our Christmas tree.
When you see these lights, you'll know why,
"The Light of the World" was born to die.
The lights remind us of His love,
And that He came from Heaven above.

Korean Child *(enters carrying paper lantern):*
My little lantern lights the way,
To where the Christians live and stay.
In Korea, our lantern shines bright
All through the Christmas Eve night.

Guatemalan Child *(enters carrying piñata):*
Guatemala is a land far, far away.
They celebrate Christmas in their own way.
A piñata is filled with candy and toys,
A stick is swung by girls and boys,
Candy and toys fall from above,
Little ones gather them with love.

Haitian Child *(enters carrying a pumpkin):*
Pumpkin soup is cooked just right,

As we eat by candlelight.
First, we bow our heads to pray
Thanking God for Christmas Day.
Then, we gather round and sing
Praises to our newborn King.

American Child *(enters carrying a small tree):*
In the United States where I come from,
This is how the Christmas celebration is done:
We place a decorated tree in a room,
Guaranteed to chase away any gloom.
The tree reminds us of a wooden cross,
Where Jesus would die for all the lost.
Whenever I see a Christmas tree,
I thank Jesus for dying for me.

Unity Child *(enters carrying dolly then places it in manger bed):*
It doesn't matter what land you come from,
The meaning of Christmas is the gift of His Son,
One tradition that will always remain
A babe in the manger, from Heaven He came.

Narrator 2: There are others who want to say,
How much they love the Lord today.
So, come on up, please don't be shy,
You love Jesus, tell us why!

(At this time in the play, we try to show that even if we are physically impaired we can still celebrate Christmas and worship the newborn King. If you have a child, or an adult, who is physically handicapped, this would be a wonderful place for her to sing a Christmas carol. It is very moving and helps the children to see that when it comes to celebrating Jesus' birthday, no one has to be left out.)

Deaf Child: Though some are deaf, they still can bring
Glorious praises to the newborn King.
(Sign "I love Jesus.")
I—*(Point thumb toward self.)*
Love—*(Cross arms over chest.)*
JESUS—*(Point to palms with middle finger.)*

Lame Child *(enters with cane):*
I am lame, there is no doubt.

But that's no reason to sit and pout.
I have a voice and I can sing
Heavenly praises to my heavenly King.
(Child sings favorite Christmas carol.)

Narrator 3: I think now you're beginning to see,
Just how "special" Christmas can be!

Blind Child *(enters with white cane)*:
It is true I've lost my sight,
Yet my heart is filled with light.
Because the Baby lying on the hay,
Has washed all my sins away!

Final Child: We want to thank you all today
For coming to our Christmas play.
Just sit tight and hold that grin,
Our "refreshments" are about to begin.
We hope you all will stay and say
That you've enjoyed our Christmas play.

NAMES

Dolores Steger

Characters and Costumes:
Chorus, dressed in Sunday school attire
Mary, dressed in robe, head scarf, sandals
Joseph, dressed in robe and sandals
Angels (two groups), dressed in white robes
Shepherds, dressed in robes and sandals
Magi, dressed in robes, sandals and crowns
Children, dressed casually

Time and Place: Shortly after Jesus' birth in the stable

Props: Gifts for Magi, chairs for Mary and Joseph

Setting: Manger scene set center stage; Mary and Joseph sit by manger; Angels, Shepherds, Magi and Children are grouped around manger.

Music: Piano/organ/choir/tape

Chorus enters stage left and moves to downstage right to music, "O Come, All Ye Faithful." Chorus speaks to audience when music stops.

Chorus *(speaking in unison):*
    God's Son is born in Bethlehem,
    And visitors with Him we'll find;
    Please join us as we ask of them
    What names for Him they have in mind.

(Music of one stanza of "Away in a Manger." Chorus speaks when music stops.)

Chorus *(in unison to Mary and Joseph):*
    Who is that baby in the stall,
    That babe of universal fame?
    What should we call Him, one and all?
    Tell, tell us that dear infant's name.
Mary and Joseph *(in unison):*
    God said to name Him Jesus, so
    We call Him sweet Emmanuel,

God with us, all the world should know,
For in Him hope and promise dwell;
But other names some will embrace;
Ask them what names they may assign
To honor Him, affirm His grace,
This miracle of God's design.

Chorus *(in unison, to Angels):*
Come, angels, tell the name you give
This child who in the stable lies,
This babe who's meant to ever live,
Who sleeps now under starry skies.

Angels *(Group 1 in unison):*
Today we call Him at His birth,
Almighty One, for now He reigns
As Ruler, Master of the earth;
His blessedness with us remains.

Angels *(Group 2, in unison):*
The gentleness upon His face,
The glow there that will never cease,
Reveals His mercy and His grace,
And so we call Him Prince of Peace.

Chorus *(in unison, to Shepherds):*
Come, shepherds on the hillsides there,
We wait for what you have to say;
What name call you the child so rare,
Who's born in Bethlehem this day?

Shepherds *(in unison):*
He'll care for flocks like shepherds do,
This baby who's so glorious;
The Lamb of God, Good Shepherd, too,
Indeed is what He is to us.

Chorus *(in unison, to Magi):*
Come, Magi who have traveled far,
Through nights that are so dark and dim,
Here guided by a brilliant star,
What name is it you've given Him?

Magi *(in unison):*
We've gold, incense and myrrh to give,
And rightfully these gifts we bring
Unto the babe who e'er will live
Above us, so we call Him King.

Chorus *(in unison, to Children):*

Come, children gathered oh so near
This baby tender, sweet and mild,
Come closer now and let us hear
The name you've given to this child.

Children (*in unison*):
We gather round the manger bed,
Protected by our God above,
Who's sent this Child with drowsy head,
Our Savior, Lord; we call Him Love.

(*Music of one stanza of "Silent Night! Holy Night!"*)

Chorus (*in unison to audience, when music stops*):
We'll praise these names; to worlds we'll tell,
As each throughout creation rings;
Love, Prince of Peace, Emmanuel,
Good Shepherd, Lamb and King of kings.

(*Music: "Go, Tell It on the Mountain" as cast takes curtain call.*)

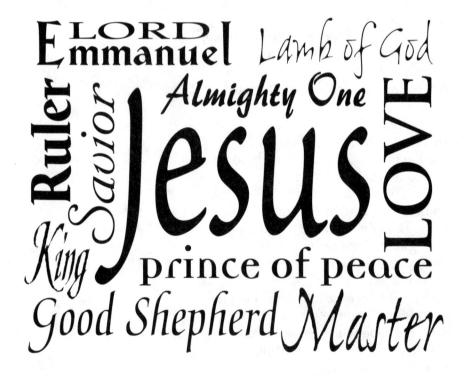

THE CHRISTMAS PLAY

Dolores Steger

Characters and Costumes:
Four Students, casually dressed
Mary, robe and head scarf
Joseph, robe
Shepherds, *(any number, three with speaking parts)* robes, must be belted;
    sandals
Wise men, robes and crowns
Angel, white robe
Reader, Sunday attire

Time: The present

Place: A church or auditorium

Setting: Manger scene is set up center stage with Mary and Joseph seated
    alongside the manger; Angel, holding a star in a raised hand, stands
    behind the manger; Four Students sit on chairs front stage right; music
    of "Away in a Manger"; Student 1 speaks when music stops.

Props: Large star for Angel, Bible for Reader, gifts for Wise men (one gift
    for Wise man 2 to contain simulated gold pieces), handkerchief for
    Joseph

Music: Choir/organ/piano/tape

Student 1: I hope our Christmas play is better this year than it was last
    year.
Student 2: How could it be any worse?
Student 1: You never know.
Student 3: Last year we tried so hard to have a perfect performance yet
    everything that could go wrong did go wrong.
Student 4: It was a total disaster.
Student 1: From beginning to end.
Student 2: I remember it well.
Others: Me too.
Student 2: The mishaps started in the very first scene.
Student 3: You are right about that! There they were, Mary and Joseph

sitting by the manger with the Angel behind them holding a star.
Student 4: And what happened?

(Angel drops star.)

Angel: Oops! I dropped the star. Sorry about that.

(Angel picks up star and resumes position holding it.)

Student 1: I heard a few people in the audience snicker.
Student 2: Could you blame them?
Student 3: The snickers became giggles when Joseph did his number.
Student 4: Oh, no. Don't remind me. The sneezes.
Joseph *(sneezing):* A-choo, a-choo, a-choo, a-choo, a-choo. Excuse me a
   minute.

(Joseph walks offstage left; returns with handkerchief, blowing nose.)

Joseph: I'm fine now. We can go on with the program.
Student 1: My face turned so red.
Student 2: I looked away. I was so embarrassed.
Student 3: I'm sure everyone in the program heard the giggling in the
   audience.
Student 4: They had to.
Student 1: And what did you think about the scene when the shepherds
   arrived?
Student 2: I could have cried.

*(Shepherds enter stage left; move slowly to manger; Shepherd 1's belt falls off;
Shepherd 2 picks up belt and taps Shepherd 1 on the shoulder.)*

Shepherd 2 *(to Shepherd 1):* Here. You dropped your belt.
Shepherd 1 *(tying belt):* How did that happen? Thanks.

(Shepherds continue toward manger; Shepherd 3, lagging behind loses a sandal.)

Shepherd 3: Hey, you guys. Wait for me. I lost my sandal.
Other Shepherds *(turning around):* Okay. We'll wait.
Shepherd 3 *(replacing sandal):* I'm all right now. Let's go.

(Shepherds continue to manger and stand around it.)

Student 4: I felt so embarrassed for those shepherds.
Student 1: I covered my eyes.
Student 2: The laughter from the audience still rings in my ears.
Student 3: That wasn't the worst of it. How about the wise men?
Student 4: All three of them. Simply a fiasco.
Other Students: Terrible.

(Wise men enter stage left; Wise man 1 and 2 carry gifts. Wise men proceed slowly to manger scene. Wise man 1's crown falls off.)

Wise man 1 *(to other Wise men)*: Stop! Stop! My crown's fallen off. I've got to get it.
Wise man 2: Okay. Okay. We'll wait.
Wise man 3: Don't get so excited.
Wise man 1 *(picking up crown and replacing on head)*: Good. I've pushed it on tight. We can go on now.

(Wise men continue slowly toward manger. Wise man 2 drops gift he's carrying and simulated gold pieces fall out.)

Wise man 2: Now I've done it. Hold everything.

(Wise men stop.)

Wise man 1: What a butterfingers!

(Wise men 1 and 3 help Wise man 2 replace the gold pieces.)

Wise man 2: Sorry about that. Glad you were here to help me.
Wise man 1: That's okay. Can we continue now?
Wise man 3: Hold on a second. I forgot my gift.
Wise man 1: You've got to be kidding.

(Wise man 3 hurries offstage left; returns with gift.)

Wise man 3 *(holding gift in outstretched hands)*: I've got it and I'm ready to go on.
Wise man 1: At last.

(Wise men proceed to manger scene and stand by it.)

Student 1: What an episode.

Student 2: I couldn't believe how the audience roared with laughter and applauded.

Student 3: I was just glad everyone finally arrived at the manger scene.

Student 4: Unfortunately, that wasn't the end of it.

Student 1: You mean at the end of the program when the Reader came out to read the Christmas story from the Bible.

Student 4: I sure do.

(Reader enters stage left carrying Bible; Reader stands front center stage and reads Luke 2:8-12. Reader then speaks to audience.)

Reader: We want to thank all of you for coming to our program. We hope you enjoyed it. And now we'd like you to join us in singing—ah— ah—ah—in singing—ah—ah—

Mary *(standing up and shouting to Reader):* "Joy to the World."

Reader: Ah, yes. Of course. "Joy to the World."

Student 4: What a mess.

Student 1: The choir had to wait for the audience to stop laughing before they began singing.

Student 2: Sad. So sad.

Student 4: I only hope Jesus knew we were trying really hard to honor Him.

Student 1: I'm sure He knew what our intentions were—what was in our hearts.

Student 3: But, you know something?

Other Students: What?

Student 3: Everyone in the audience had a good time. They laughed and clapped and clapped and laughed. I've never seen so much joy at any of our other Christmas programs.

Other Students: So?

Student 3: So, isn't that what Christmas is all about? Joy. Joy for the birth of Jesus and for the joy He puts in our hearts.

Student 1: I never thought about it that way.

Student 2: Me neither.

Student 4: You do have a point. Maybe we should wish for some glitches in our Christmas program this year.

Student 1: Let's not.

Other Students: No. Let's not.

(Music: "Joy to the World" as cast comes forward for curtain call.)

WHERE IS THE CHRIST CHILD TONIGHT?

June Gordon

Characters and Costumes:
There are two main speaking parts as follows:
Narrator (teen or adult)—wearing casual dress
Young Minister (adult or older teenage boy)—suit and tie
Other Participants (in order of appearance):
Cherub Choir—kindergarten through third grade
Third Graders
Kindergarteners
Carillon Choir—through junior high
First Graders
Second Graders
Prekindergarteners
Mary and Joseph
Innkeeper
Three or four shepherds
Three wise men
Congregation of church—thirteen to fifteen members of adult choir
Duet
Soloist
Modern-day mother, father and baby or doll

Introduction of Participants and staging instructions:
Program proceeds through children's parts, into a small church scene using adult actors; ending with manger scene, together with modern-day mother, father and baby.

Stage Props:
1. Manger with star above it and bale of straw beside it, placed on right side of stage three to four feet from front and toward edge of stage. Manger (with baby) will be moved back and toward center (though not completely centered, as modern-day family share stage) before last scene.
2. Small Podium—facing the audience, some feet behind manger on same side. Narrator uses podium for program; when he leaves stage he turns the podium to face other side of stage, and moves it farther back from manger.
3. Thirteen to fifteen folding chairs—to be placed quickly facing small podium for the "Happy Valley" congregation. Chairs to be folded and

set aside (leaving one) before last scene.
4. Sign "Happy Valley Church" to be placed center of stage facing audience; removed before last scene.
5. Cherub Choir seated offstage—right side of stage
6. Carillon Choir seated offstage—left side of stage
7. Adult Choir—sits offstage behind Cherub Choir

(Please note: Success of the program will be dependent upon having very good speakers for the Narrator and Minister. The Narrator reads his part, but it would be more effective if the Minister could speak from memory—except for Scripture.)

Narrator: On television some years ago
A question was always asked
After the late-night show:
"Where is your child tonight"?
But we want to present to you
A question with a different view:
"Where is the Christ child tonight"?
We rush and rush till Christmas is through,
Cards, presents, parties—so much to do!
But we hope in our songs and verse you'll find
The Christ child's manger—and peace of mind!

Cherub Choir: "Away in a Manger" *(remain seated offstage)*

Narrator: Now our third graders wish to welcome you.
Third Graders *(coming to stage and speaking as a group):*
Welcome
We're so happy to see each face tonight,
And we hope every heart is happy and light,
Blessed with love and holiday cheer—
'Cause Christ's birthday is drawing near.
And we hope you'll be glad you took the time
To come and listen to our songs and rhymes.
And we hope your Christmas will be more bright
Because we've praised God for His love this night.
(They return to seats in Cherub Choir.)
Narrator: Now our kindergarteners want to tell you
The most important thing to do:
Kindergarteners *(coming to stage and speaking as a group):*

Give Thanks

Christmas is coming soon, you see,
And everyone's happy as can be.
But let's not forget, in our fun
To thank God for His Son!
(They return to seats in Cherub Choir.)

Narrator: Next our Carillon Choir wants to say in song
How Jesus does, in love, to us all belong!

Carillon Choir: "Some Children See Him" *(words by Wihla Hutson, music
by Alfred S. Burt © Hollis Music, Inc. Children stay seated offstage.)*

Narrator: It's our first graders turn to have their say
About what should be done for Christmas Day.
First Graders *(coming to stage and speaking as a group):*

The Christmas Rush

Why—oh—why is everyone so busy?
Running around in such a tizzy!
We think they better slow down a bit—
And take time to enjoy the Christmas Spirit!
(They return to seats in Cherub Choir.)
Narrator: Now our second graders want to tell you
What they think of Christmas too.
Second Graders *(coming to stage and speaking as a group):*

Sharing Christmas

We wish and hope for so many things
Our moms say we make their heads ring!
And our moms also say whatever we get
We must remember to share it!
Narrator: Our smaller angels had a problem tonight too,
Trying to decide how to best honor Him;
And they've decided they will share with you
Something very special to them.
Perhaps at one time you had one too,
A little stuffed animal—your special friend!

*(Prekindergarten Children come to stage with their favorite stuffed animals,
holding them high for the audience to see, before they return to their parents.)*

Narrator: God, too, had a special animal friend you see—
That night so long ago—a little gray donkey.

And Joseph, with Mary on the donkey, searched that night,
For a warm place to rest from their weary plight;
Just any shelter out of the cold and the snow,
But the innkeepers frowned—and all said, "No!"

(Mary and Joseph come onto stage from one side, and Innkeeper enters from opposite side; they pantomine conversation.)

Narrator: Until at last one innkeeper said,
"I have no room—but perhaps in my barn—
The hay is clean—you could make a bed."

(Mary and Joseph go to sit on straw by manger; Innkeeper leaves.)

Carillon Choir: "No Room" *(They remain seated to sing.)*
Narrator: And Mary brought forth her firstborn Son,
The promised Messiah—God's chosen One;
And the rough straw of the manger bed—
Formed the pillow for His tiny head,
And shepherds out in the fields so cold
Were frightened a heavenly host to behold!

Adult Choir: "While Shepherds Watched Their Flocks" *(All verses. They remain seated to sing as Shepherds come to kneel at manger.)*

Narrator: And nothing could compare with the shepherds' joy,
When they found that precious baby boy;
But others knew in a far distant land,
For as they studied the sky they saw God's hand
In the heavens place a new star so bright,
And they had to follow that clear pure light,
Bearing gifts for God's only Son
Our chosen Messiah—the Holy One.

Adult Choir: "We Three Kings of Orient Are" *(First verse only. Choir remains seated to sing, and Wise men enter to place gifts and kneel by manger.)*

Narrator: A simple story so often told,
Something that happened so long ago.
Why does it speak to our hearts as it did then?
Is the babe still wishing for a place to come in?

What has happened to this Christ child tonight?
Has His birth been lost in silver tinsel so bright?
When He speaks to our hearts—do we turn Him away?
Saying, "Sorry Lord—no place here to stay!"

(Narrator moves podium back a few feet on the stage; turning on an angle to face other side of stage, rather than the audience. Then, Narrator, Mary, Joseph, Shepherds and Wise men leave stage as stage helpers quickly place thirteen to fifteen folding chairs facing podium, and a sign "Happy Valley Church" is placed on floor facing audience.)

Minister *(entering with Bible in hand, which he places on podium; he doesn't speak until congregation has filed in, taking seats):* Good morning! It is certainly good to see so many this morning! It must be because Christmas is coming. I do believe we have over a dozen! Of course, we have over one hundred on the roll—but still this is much better than the six we had last Sunday. Praise the Lord!

Member of Congregation: Amen!

Minister: For our special this morning I have asked the Armstrong brothers to sing "Since Jesus Came Into My Heart."

Duet *(rising and standing by piano):* "Since Jesus Came Into My Heart"

Minister: Thank you, boys, for that fine number. I asked you to sing that song because I wanted to speak along those lines today. And about the fact that, even as Jesus was born as a little baby in a manger long ago, He must be spiritually born in our hearts today. When we accept Jesus into our hearts, then we individually are reborn from a world ruled by sin into a spiritual world, where we are God's children! In the third chapter of the Gospel of John, beginning with verse 1, we read: *(Minister reads John 3:1-16, then pauses a moment before continuing.)*

Minister: So, in closing I would like for each one to ask himself—as we celebrate Christ's birth on earth—if we have ever allowed Him to be born spiritually in our own hearts. For by accepting Christ as our Savior, we are "born again" ourselves—and we will know the joy the shepherds knew so long ago when they accepted the tiny babe and believed He was their Messiah. *(Pauses a moment then continues.)* Now, if you will please turn in your books to page ___, we will end our service with the song "Heaven Came Down and Glory Filled My Soul."

Happy Valley Congregation: "Heaven Came Down and Glory Filled My Soul" *(words and music by John Peterson, © Singspiration, Inc.)*

(As song ends, Minister turns podium back toward audience and removes "Happy Valley Church" sign, as congregation folds the chairs, leaving one for last scene, centered on the left side of stage; manger and bale of straw are centered on right side. Narrator returns to podium on stage, and Mary and Joseph return to manger; and a young mother and father with small baby come, for mother to sit with baby on chair, with the father standing behind.)

Narrator *(speaking after characters are in place):* So—as we all know—
On that starry night so long ago,
God, His only Son did give—
So according to His plan,
Our babies may forever live!

Soloist *(standing by piano):* "O Holy Night!"

Narrator: I pray tonight God's love we have all believed
And have the gift of His Son received.
Now, from the back of your bulletin, let's sing
May our praises make the heavens ring!

Congregation and All Actors: "Joy to the World" *(one verse only)*
Narrator: So as our program ends this wonderful season
Ofttimes so busy we forget its reason;
We hope perhaps we have had a small part—
In helping you find the Christ child—as you looked in your heart!

(A moment of silence.)

Narrator: Will every one please stand and sing
Quietly, reverently, "Silent Night,"
Honoring our Savior and King.
Then remain standing for our minister to bless us
And may we all have a spiritually filled Christmas!
Minister: Benediction

(Notes: "Joy to the World" (one verse) and "Silent Night! Holy Night!" should be printed on the back of the Christmas program bulletin. Also, I have indicated that all singers should remain seated, excepting duet and soloist, in order to expedite the theme of the program, and avoid confusion. However, of course, this will be dependent upon your church's seating arrangements and the acoustics.)

United Nations publications of related interest

The following UN publications may be obtained from the addresses indicated below, or at your local distributor:

Yearbook of the United Nations, Vol. 50
E.97.I.1 90-411-1042-9 1996 1552 pp. $150.00

Basic Facts About the United Nations
E.98.I.20 92-1-100793-3 350 pp. $10.00

The Blue Helmets: A Review of United Nations Peacekeeping
E.96.I.14 92-1-100611-2 808 pp. $29.95

World Economic and Social Survey 1998
E.98.II.C.1 92-1-109134-9 180 pp. $24.95

The World's Women 1970-1995: Trends and Statistics
Second Edition
E.95.XVII.2 92-1-161372-8 202 pp. $15.95

UN Briefing Papers: The World Conferences—Developing Priorities for the 21st Century
E.97.I.5 92-1-100631-7 112 pp. $12.00

UN Briefing Papers: Human Rights Today—A United Nations Priority
E.98.I.22 92-1-100797-6 85 pp.

An Agenda for Development
E.98.I.3 92-1-100644-9 110 pp. $7.50

Statistical Yearbook, 42nd Edition
B.97.XVII.1 92-1-061174-8 946 pp. $120.00

United Nations Publications
2 United Nations Plaza
Room DC2-853
New York, NY 10017
United States
Tel: (212) 963-8302, (800) 253-9646
Fax: (212) 963-3489

United Nations Publications
Sales Office and Bookshop
CH-1211 Geneva 10
Switzerland
Tel: 41 (22) 917-26-13, 917-26-14
Fax: 41 (22) 917-00-27

Partnerships for Global Community · 1998

Kofi A. Annan
Secretary-General of the United Nations

Partnerships for Global Community

Annual Report on the Work of the Organization

1998

United Nations

Published by the United Nations
Department of Public Information
New York, 10017

United Nations Sales No. E.99.I.3
ISBN 92-1-100798-4
Litho in United Nations, New York

Contents

Introduction

1. Nearly a decade has passed since the end of the cold war, but the contours of the new era remain poorly understood. Nations large and small are grappling with new responsibilities and new constraints. Unpredictability and surprise have become almost commonplace. Uncertainty exists, in some cases even anxiety, about new roles that may be required of multilateral organizations, and more broadly about their place in the international community. Indeed, the peoples of the United Nations, in whose name the Charter is written, are searching for new ways to define how they are united in community though divided by custom and conviction, power and interests.

2. Notwithstanding the extraordinary achievements of multilateralism during the past half-century, too many voices remain unheard, too much pain persists and too many additional opportunities for human betterment are forgone for us to rest satisfied with the way things work today. These still unmet challenges must remain uppermost on the United Nations agenda. The Millennium Assembly to be held in September 2000 affords a unique opportunity for the world's leaders to look beyond their pressing daily concerns and consider what kind of United Nations they can envision and will support in the new century.

3. To facilitate those deliberations, I propose to submit a report to the Millennium Assembly, suggesting to Member States a set of workable objectives and institutional means for the United Nations to meet the challenges of human solidarity in the years ahead. The report will draw on several reviews of recent United Nations conferences

scheduled between now and then. It will also benefit from the diverse views and aspirations expressed at a series of global and regional hearings and seminars that I propose to convene—global town meetings, in effect—and which many individual Governments, civil society actors and other groups are also holding.

4.   The "quiet revolution" of institutional reforms that I initiated last year was intended to revitalize an organizational machinery that in some respects had been made sluggish and creaky by the effects of the cold war and the North-South confrontation, and to better position it for the highly complex, increasingly interconnected and far more fluid context of the new era. I can say with some satisfaction that the United Nations family today acts with greater unity of purpose and coherence of effort than it did a year ago. The new teamwork is most pronounced within the Secretariat and in its relations with the programmes and funds.

5.   The work programme has been organized in four core areas: peace and security, development cooperation, international economic and social affairs, and humanitarian affairs; a fifth, human rights, is designated a cross-cutting issue. In each cluster, an Executive Committee now manages common, cross-cutting and overlapping policy concerns.

6.   To integrate the work of the Executive Committees and address matters affecting the Organization as a whole, a cabinet-style Senior Management Group, comprising the leadership from the various United Nations headquarters, has been established. It meets weekly, with members in Geneva, Vienna, Nairobi and Rome participating through teleconferencing. A Strategic Planning Unit has been established to enable the Group to consider individual questions on its agenda within broader and longer-term frames of reference. Member States approved my recommendation

to create the post of Deputy Secretary-General; in the few short months that Louise Frechette of Canada has occupied this office, it has been demonstrated conclusively how critical it is in augmenting the leadership and management capacity of the Secretariat.

7.   The Secretariat itself has been streamlined, through the merging and elimination of units; nearly a thousand posts have been cut, to fewer than 9,000; and the budget has been reduced to less than that of the previous biennium. A task force on human resources management that I convened earlier this year has just submitted its report to me; I will act expeditiously and decisively on its recommendations.

8.   Productive working relations within the United Nations system as a whole, including the Bretton Woods institutions, have been expanded and deepened through the Administrative Committee on Coordination. Several concrete instances are documented in this report.

9.   In my reform programme, I also recommended that Member States refine or revise a number of institutional practices under their jurisdiction. In the main, the General Assembly decided to defer its consideration of such questions or continue them at the fifty-third session. Still to be approved is the proposal that specific time limits be adopted for all new mandates, a relatively simple procedure that would significantly enhance the effectiveness of programme activities and the General Assembly's own oversight role. The proposal to adopt a results-based budget system also remains under review. This initiative is of the utmost importance, because no single measure would do more to increase accountability and efficiency in the work of the Organization. Member States are also still studying details of the proposed Development Account, an instrument by which savings from

administrative efficiencies would be invested in innovative developing projects.

10.   Lastly, as part of the endeavour to reinvigorate the United Nations I have made a particular effort to establish a mutually beneficial dialogue with the international business community. Business has a stake in the soft infrastructure that the United Nations system produces—the norms, standards and best practices on which the smooth flow of international transactions depends. Moreover, business is increasingly coming to appreciate that the work of the United Nations on behalf of peace, human rights and development helps lay the stable foundations that the expansion of its own opportunities requires. In turn, the United Nations appreciates that business has the capital, technology and expertise necessary to fuel economic growth, and that its attitude and readiness to cooperate can critically affect the prospects of a wide variety of other objectives. The dialogue is accordingly premised on my conviction that expanding markets and human security can and should go hand in hand.

11.   Engagement with the business community parallels the long-standing and increasingly close working relationships the United Nations has with non-governmental organizations. Whether in human rights or the environment, in development, humanitarian assistance or arms limitation, non-governmental organizations are indispensable partners for United Nations efforts at the country level and, in some cases, at policy levels as well. In short, the United Nations is both witness to and participant in the birth of a global civil society.

12.   Not long after I proposed my reform agenda to the General Assembly in the summer of 1997, Mr. Ted Turner, Co-Chairman of Time Warner Inc., announced his extraordinary gift of $1 billion to support United Nations

programmes. Never before in the history of philanthropy had a single gift of such magnitude been given for this or any other cause. The necessary institutional arrangements to administer the gift are now in place, and the first set of grants, totalling some $22 million, have been allocated. The majority of projects funded in this first round were in the areas of children's health, family planning and reproductive health, as well as environmental and climate change. The United Nations Fund for International Partnerships has been established within the Secretariat to manage the process of grant allocation and ensure that it remains fully consistent with the Organization's priorities.

13.   This unprecedented act of generosity not only makes available new and additional resources for United Nations work on behalf of the world's most vulnerable people and its fragile planetary life support systems. It is also an expression of an entirely new phenomenon: an incipient sense of global citizenship and responsibility.

14.   Another sign of change in the global arena this past year was the conclusion of negotiations on the Convention banning anti-personnel landmines and the Statute of the International Criminal Court. Governments conducted the actual negotiations in both cases, and groups of so-called like-minded States provided the core support that led to their adoption; but in both instances a new expression of global people power was manifest: individuals and groups animated by humanitarian and human rights concerns, united by the Internet and supported by world public opinion.

15.   One of the most profound challenges that we face as a community of nations is to understand better the emerging socio-economic forces and forms of globalization, to shape them to serve our needs and to respond effectively to their deleterious consequences. There is a

great deal of talk today about life in the global village. If that village is to be a truly desirable place for all of us on this planet, it must be embedded in and guided by broadly shared values and principles; its policing functions and the provision of other public goods must be strengthened and made more predictable; and a bridge must be constructed between, in effect, the Dow Jones index and the human development index.

16.   No organization in the world is better suited to contribute to these ends than the United Nations, because no other enjoys its scope and legitimacy; but to move forward we need to shed baggage, create new visions and devise new ways to achieve them. We have taken the first vital steps towards transformation, but we have some way to go before we become a truly effective twenty-first-century organization. Over the next two years, leading up to the Millennium Assembly, I shall solicit the views of Member States, civil society actors and other interested groups and individuals on the best way to get from here to there.

1 Achieving peace and security

17.   The world has been mercifully free from large-scale regional conflict over the past 12 months. Many local wars have continued, however, and new ones have broken out, including, for the first time in this decade, a war over territory between two neighbouring States, Eritrea and Ethiopia. While there have been some important successes for the international community, including the restoration of the democratically elected Government in Sierra Leone, peace in many parts of the world remains precarious. Moreover, peace processes in several regions, including some to which the United Nations has devoted extensive resources over a long period, show a distressing tendency to unravel.

18.   Of particular concern is the lack of progress in the Middle East peace process; the turmoil in Afghanistan; the escalation of violence in Kosovo (Federal Republic of Yugoslavia); the ongoing civil war in the Sudan; the continuing instability and violence in the Democratic Republic of the Congo and the rest of the Great Lakes region; and the return to civil war in Angola. Our efforts in Angola were dealt a severe blow when my Special Representative, Alioune Blondin Beye, was tragically killed in a plane crash on 26 June, together with seven others. The rising tensions between India and Pakistan over Kashmir and other issues is also a major cause of concern, as is the stalemated peace process in Cyprus.

19.   The adoption, late in 1997, of the Ottawa Convention on the Prohibition of the Use, Stockpiling, Production and Transfer of Anti-personnel Mines and on Their Destruction was an unprecedented achievement. By 31

July 1998, the Convention had been signed by 128 countries and ratified by 30. It is expected to enter into force early next year. Several important States still feel unable to sign it, however, and combatants in several wars continue to use these barbaric weapons. Even where they have ceased doing so, millions of mines planted in earlier years remain in place. They will continue to kill and maim innocent men, women and children for decades.

20.   Similarly, the adoption of the Statute of the International Criminal Court at Rome in July, a historic development in the age-long struggle to punish and deter war crimes, has yet to win universal acceptance. Even on the most optimistic assumption it will be some years before the Court begins to discharge its functions. Meanwhile, deplorable acts of brutality continue to be reported from many parts of the world, and all too often the culprits go unpunished.

21.   Nor is the human race yet delivered from the threat of nuclear annihilation. In fact we are at a critical moment in the history of efforts to reduce this danger. The successes of previous years, the indefinite extension of the Treaty on the Non-Proliferation of Nuclear Weapons and the signing of the Comprehensive Nuclear-Test-Ban Treaty, have been called into question this year by the decision of two non-signatories, India and Pakistan, to conduct underground nuclear tests. This has increased the tensions between those two countries and given the world a sombre reminder that non-proliferation cannot be taken for granted.

22.   Hardly less alarming is the threat posed by chemical and biological weapons. Here, I am glad to report that in the past year more States have renounced the development and use of the former, while the Convention banning the latter is being gradually strengthened through

efforts to elaborate a verification protocol. The fact that some States may be stocking or developing such weapons clandestinely remains a serious threat to world peace, however.

23.   The world lived through a period of high tension in February when Iraq seemed set on refusing to comply with its disarmament obligations, and some Member States prepared for military action to enforce compliance. War was averted only by the timely collective action of the international community.

24.   The Memorandum of Understanding, which I and Deputy Prime Minister Tariq Aziz signed on 23 February, was an effective demonstration of preventive diplomacy. If fully implemented it would set a valuable precedent, proving that by united action the world can indeed prevent conflict, as the founders of the Organization intended. Unfortunately, the situation in Iraq still appears to be far from resolution.

Prevention

25.   Article 1 of the Charter of the United Nations calls for effective collective measures for the prevention and removal of threats to the peace. Conflict prevention, therefore, should be one of the Organization's deepest commitments, yet there is still too little emphasis on preventive action. Instead, vast resources are spent on efforts to "cure" conflicts, when for many of the victims it is already too late.

26.   Preventing potential conflicts from crossing the threshold of violence requires early warning of situations with the potential for crisis, proper analysis, an integrated preventive strategy, and the political will and resources to implement such a strategy.

27.   In some cases effective prevention is actually impeded by the traditional focus on external threats to a State's security. Today we recognize that many other threats to human security, such as natural disasters, ethnic tension and human rights violations, may also be sources of conflict. The intimate relationship between social justice, material well-being and peace must also be taken into account if action is to be pursued far enough to prevent local conflicts from escalating and spilling over into the international arena.

28.   In its work at the field level, the United Nations has already started to embrace a new holistic concept of security. Its efforts to reduce poverty and promote development and democratization—including electoral assistance and civic education—have gradually become more comprehensive and more integrated. All of these efforts may be described as preventive peace-building, since they attack the root causes of many conflicts.

29.   If then the determinants of human security include the economic, social and humanitarian prerequisites of human well-being and stability, should not the role of the Security Council also be broadened? Can the Council seriously aspire to making prevention the norm rather than the exception unless it engages with the economic and social developments that influence peace and security with the same energy and seriousness with which it tackles the political ones? Such an approach would imply new forms of cooperation between the Security Council, the General Assembly and the Economic and Social Council, as well as between all the organs of the United Nations and the Member States.

30.   Under the Charter, there is a dormant provision that the Economic and Social Council may furnish information and assistance to the Security Council upon a request

from the latter (Article 65). As the Security Council is increasingly required to address economic, social and humanitarian crises that threaten global security, it may wish to consider invoking this mechanism. This could help to achieve better communication and coordination between organs of the United Nations whose primary focus is on economic, social and humanitarian affairs.

Diplomacy

31. The role of diplomacy is so central to virtually all United Nations activities that its specific contribution is sometimes overlooked. That is especially true of successful preventive diplomacy. A former Under-Secretary-General once remarked to a television producer who asked where he could make a film about conflict prevention, "If you can film it, it probably is not working!" Indeed, the light of publicity is often turned on only when conflict has become entrenched; and that in itself often makes compromise more difficult, since leaders fear that concessions made in public will be interpreted as weakness by opponents, or as betrayal by supporters. One does not always have the choice, however. My journey to Baghdad in February was undoubtedly an exercise in preventive diplomacy, but I could not possibly have accomplished it unnoticed.

32. During the past year, often in difficult and sometimes dangerous conditions, the United Nations has been engaged in the sensitive diplomacy of peacemaking, where success in preventing conflict often goes unremarked. I have appointed prominent and skilled diplomats, from the international community as well as the United Nations, to serve as my personal representatives in situations of actual

or potential conflict. Their tasks have ranged from information-gathering to mediation.

33. While United Nations missions have achieved notable successes, there are some conflicts where hostility is so intense and distrust so pervasive that no amount of skilful diplomacy will achieve a breakthrough. That has been the case in Afghanistan during the past year. Despite the meetings held in New York by the group of eight concerned countries, and the best efforts of the United Nations Special Mission to Afghanistan, the warring Afghan parties have continued to pursue the military option at great humanitarian cost. They have also refused to participate in any meaningful dialogue. In this, they have been regrettably aided and encouraged by outside Powers.

34. Many of the most sensitive and difficult diplomatic initiatives of the United Nations during the year have been undertaken in Africa's trouble spots. In May, in view of continuing violence in the Great Lakes region of Central Africa, I urged the leaders of Burundi and Rwanda to redouble their efforts to build stable peace, national unity and respect for human rights.

35. In the Democratic Republic of the Congo, I was compelled to withdraw the United Nations investigative team earlier this year because of persistent non-cooperation and harassment from the authorities. I subsequently called on regional Governments to acknowledge the team's findings, which, among other things, raised the possibility that some of the reported violations of human rights could have constituted genocide. I also drew attention to the need for substantial international assistance to help achieve stability in the region.

36. Throughout the year, the United Nations has been assisting the mediator for Burundi, Mwalimu Julius Nyerere, while the establishment of the Office of my Rep-

resentative in Nairobi will enhance the Organization's capacity for preventive action in the subregion as a whole.

37. On the contentious issue of East Timor, real progress has been made during the year: an important breakthrough was achieved at the meeting I convened in New York in August between the Foreign Ministers of Indonesia and Portugal. For the first time since 1975 the prospects for an agreed resolution of the conflict between the East Timorese and Indonesia are hopeful.

38. Earlier this year a new United Nations Political Office was established in Bougainville, the first United Nations political mission to the South Pacific. The quiet diplomacy of peacemaking has also been pursued during the past year in the Middle East, South Asia, Angola, Cambodia, Cyprus, Somalia and Western Sahara.

39. Perhaps the most delicate kind of preventive diplomacy is that which seeks to bring about reconciliation between antagonistic political forces within a country, in the hope of preventing or resolving conflicts which, if left to escalate, might in time become a direct threat to international peace and security. This was the purpose of my mission to Nigeria at the end of June. In such cases, an invitation from the Government of the Member State concerned is an essential prerequisite for involvement.

40. Another sensitive mission was the information-gathering panel of eminent personalities that visited Algeria at my request in July and August. It was made possible by an invitation from the Government of Algeria.

41. Since the causes of conflict are usually regional or local, I believe that regional organizations are particularly well suited to play an important role in early warning and preventive diplomacy. Therefore I am seeking, in the spirit of Chapter VIII of the Charter, to create a real partnership, with a more rational and cost-effective division of

labour, between those organizations and the United Nations. This year I established a United Nations liaison office at the headquarters of the Organization of African Unity in Addis Ababa. We also continued to consolidate our links with the Organization for Security and Cooperation in Europe. In July I invited the heads of regional organizations to a meeting in New York to discuss concrete steps we can take to improve our cooperation in preventing conflict.

42. The collaboration of the United Nations with regional and subregional organizations also illustrates the close relationship between peace-building, development and disarmament. The Organization has helped members of the United Nations Standing Advisory Committee on Security Questions in Central Africa in their efforts to build peace and security in that subregion. The United Nations Regional Centre for Peace and Disarmament in Asia and the Pacific has provided a valuable forum for meetings on regional confidence- and security-building measures. I trust that the recent decision to strengthen the regional centres in Lomé and Lima will lead to similar activity throughout Africa and Latin America.

Preventive deployment

43. Peacekeeping can be a valuable tool for conflict prevention. Peacekeeping forces are generally deployed only after, or during, a conflict, usually under the terms of a ceasefire agreement, their main task being to prevent violence from flaring up again. From there, intellectually, it is only a small step to the deployment of forces to prevent violence from breaking out in the first place, in situations where there is an obvious danger of that happening. Unfortunately, preventive deployment confronts many political

obstacles. In general, only the spectacle of actual violence, with all its tragic consequences, convinces the parties to the conflict, potential troop-contributing countries and the Security Council of the utility or necessity of deploying a peacekeeping force.

44. Late in 1992, the Security Council did, however, take the unprecedented decision to establish a presence of the United Nations Protection Force in the former Yugoslav Republic of Macedonia, as a preventive measure. The force deployed, the United Nations Preventive Deployment Force (UNPREDEP), remains the sole example of a purely preventive United Nations force. The experiment must be counted as a success, inasmuch as war has so far been avoided in the former Yugoslav Republic of Macedonia despite considerable tensions both between it and its neighbours and between different ethnic groups within the Republic. While no one can guarantee that this relatively favourable state of affairs will continue, the presence of UNPREDEP has undoubtedly had a positive effect, helping to defuse tensions both within the country and in the wider region. This year's crisis in Kosovo underlined the vital role of UNPREDEP in preserving stability. I am consequently glad to report that on 21 July 1998 the Security Council decided, on my recommendation, to authorize an increase in the troop strength of UNPREDEP and to extend its current mandate for a period of six months, until 28 February 1999.

Disarmament

45. My vision of the Organization places disarmament near the centre of its mission of peace and development. I am therefore delighted that the General Assembly

supported my decision to re-establish the Department for Disarmament Affairs with an Under-Secretary-General as its head. The Assembly also acted on my recommendation that it review the work of the Disarmament Commission and the First Committee with a view to updating, revitalizing and streamlining their work. Once that task is completed, the reform proposals for the disarmament sector of the Organization will have been fully implemented.

46. The essential role of the United Nations in this area is one of norm-setting and of strengthening and consolidating multilateral principles for disarmament. When we consider how such principles, norms and procedures have fared over the past year, we see a mixed picture, however.

47. We are at a critical moment in the history of efforts to reduce the danger posed by nuclear weapons. Any increase in the number of nuclear-weapon States will have serious implications for peace and security. It is therefore of the utmost importance that the Comprehensive Nuclear-Test-Ban Treaty, together with the objectives agreed to at the 1995 Review and Extension Conference of the Parties to the Treaty on the Non-Proliferation of Nuclear Weapons, become universally accepted. Positive developments this year include the issuance of the eight-nation joint declaration on creating a nuclear-weapon-free world, and the establishment of two ad hoc committees in the Conference on Disarmament. One committee will negotiate with a view to reaching agreement on effective international arrangements to assure non-nuclear-weapon States against the use or threat of use of nuclear weapons; the other will negotiate a treaty banning the production of fissile material for nuclear explosive devices.

48. The new review process of the Non-Proliferation Treaty is now in place, and two nuclear-weapon States have ratified the Test-Ban Treaty. In the past year, efforts were

also made to consolidate existing nuclear-weapon-free zones, notably those in Africa and in South-East Asia, and to move towards the establishment of another such zone in Central Asia.

49.   In the light of the expectation that the international community would take concrete steps towards the further reduction of nuclear weapons, the underground nuclear tests conducted by India and Pakistan were a highly disturbing development. I have urged those States to refrain from any further nuclear testing, to adhere immediately to the Test-Ban Treaty, to refrain from deploying nuclear weapons, and to freeze their weapons development programmes, as well as the development of missiles capable of delivering nuclear weapons.

50.   In the struggle for sustainable peace and development, especially in subregions where State structures are fragile, steps need to be taken to curb the flow of small arms circulating in civil society. It is estimated that 90 per cent of those killed or wounded by light military weapons are civilians and, most shockingly, that 80 per cent of those are women and children.

51.   One approach to this problem would be to seek to build a global consensus on monitoring and controlling illicit arms transfers and their links with trafficking in other contraband goods. The holding of a United Nations conference on all aspects of the illicit arms trade in the near future would be an important step in that direction. In 1997, the Inter-American Convention against the Illicit Manufacturing of and Trafficking in Firearms, Ammunition, Explosives and Other Related Materials was signed, establishing an essential mechanism in the area of arms regulation. I also welcome the initiative taken by the Economic Community of West African States in preparing for a moratorium on the import, export and manufacture of small arms.

52.   In pursuing our goal of disarmament, efforts to reduce the supply of weapons are not enough; reduction in the demand for them is equally, if not more, important.

53.   The amended Protocol II to the Convention on Certain Conventional Weapons—a partial ban on land-mines—will enter into force in December 1998, and the Ottawa Convention—a comprehensive ban—is expected to enter into force early in 1999. It is crucial to ensure adherence to one or both of these instruments by as many States as possible, and to support the negotiation of a ban on exports in the Conference on Disarmament.

54.   The Department for Disarmament Affairs also plays a critical role in post-conflict peace-building, notably in the collection, disposal and destruction of weapons and in the reintegration of former combatants into civil society. Our efforts must always be set in the context of the broader work of the Organization aimed at preventing and resolving conflicts, and at building cultures which reject violence.

55.   Finally, wider commitment to greater openness and transparency in military matters would make a valuable contribution to confidence-building and creating security at lower levels of armaments. There are already two instruments for this purpose: the United Nations Register of Conventional Arms and the system for standardized reporting of military expenditures. I look to Member States to increase and improve their participation in both of these, and I am committed to giving them whatever assistance I can.

Peacekeeping

56.   Over the past year, I am pleased to note that the international community has begun to overcome its reluctance to make use of the Organization's peacekeeping

capacity. The Security Council has authorized two new operations: the United Nations Mission in the Central African Republic (MINURCA) and the United Nations Observer Mission in Sierra Leone (UNOMSIL).

57. United Nations peacekeeping clearly offers certain unique advantages not to be found elsewhere, including the universality of its mandate and the breadth of its experience. If the Security Council is known to be ready to authorize new peacekeeping operations whenever, and for as long as, they may be needed, this will not only strengthen the United Nations conflict-prevention efforts but also assist its wider peacemaking and post-conflict peace-building endeavours.

58. Fifty years after the establishment of the first United Nations peacekeeping operation, there are today some 14,500 military and police personnel deployed in missions around the globe under the United Nations flag. Peacekeeping continues to be adapted to changing needs and cooperation with regional organizations is now an important aspect. Although caution and judgement are required before deciding on joint operations, such cooperation can bring together the motivation and knowledge of local actors with the legitimacy, expertise and resources of the world Organization.

59. At Headquarters, the Department of Peacekeeping Operations has continued its efforts to strengthen the Organization's capacity to respond swiftly. This past year has seen some progress in the development of the United Nations standby arrangements system, which now includes 74 Member States, with over 100,000 personnel pledged in the framework of the system. I welcome in particular the increased interest in these developments shown by African States. The Department continues to work with Member States on the enhancement of Africa's peacekeeping capacity.

60. Within the context of the standby arrangements system, I was pleased to attend the inauguration of the headquarters of the United Nations Standby Forces High Readiness Brigade in Copenhagen in September 1997. I have also requested, but not yet received, funding for posts necessary to create a rapidly deployable mission headquarters.

61. The total number of peacekeepers in the field has declined since the early 1990s, as a consequence of the winding down of several major United Nations operations, but the actual number of United Nations peacekeeping operations has in fact risen from 15 to 17 in the past year. Six of these are in Europe, four in the Middle East, four in Africa, two in Asia and one in the Americas. Under the auspices of the Department of Political Affairs, the United Nations also maintains a human rights and judicial reform mission in Guatemala.

Sanctions

62. I have in the past underlined the need for a mechanism that renders sanctions a less blunt and more effective instrument. Therefore, I welcome the fact that the concept of "smart sanctions", which seek to pressure regimes rather than peoples and thus reduce humanitarian costs, has been gaining support among Member States. The increasing interest in more targeted sanctions was evident in the recent measures applied by the Security Council against the military junta in Sierra Leone and against UNITA in Angola.

63. Resolutions covering mandatory measures should also address humanitarian exemptions and third-State issues. Although sanctions regimes established by the

Security Council normally do include humanitarian exemptions, some human rights treaty-monitoring bodies have stressed the need for such regimes to include specific measures protecting the human rights of vulnerable groups. The Committee on Economic, Social and Cultural Rights has argued that such considerations must be fully taken into account when a sanctions regime is being designed; that effective monitoring must be undertaken throughout the period when sanctions are in force; and that the party or parties responsible for the imposition, maintenance or implementation of sanctions should take steps to prevent any disproportionate suffering being experienced by vulnerable groups within the targeted country. The Committee on the Rights of the Child took a similar approach, pointing out that, in certain conditions, sanctions can act as an obstacle to the implementation of the Convention on the Rights of the Child.

64.   The international community should be under no illusion: these humanitarian and human rights policy goals cannot easily be reconciled with those of a sanctions regime. It cannot be too strongly emphasized that sanctions are a tool of enforcement and, like other methods of enforcement, they will do harm. This should be borne in mind when the decision to impose them is taken, and when the results are subsequently evaluated.

Post-conflict peace-building

65.   Post-conflict peace-building involves integrated and coordinated actions aimed at addressing the root causes of violence—whether political, legal, institutional, military, humanitarian, human rights–related, environmental, economic and social, cultural or demographic—

and laying the foundations for a durable peace. Post-conflict peace-building may be seen as a long-term conflict prevention strategy. Because the causes of conflicts differ, United Nations actions must be tailored to specific situations to strengthen the peace process and make it irreversible. There is no standard post-conflict peace-building model.

66.   The largest and arguably most important United Nations peace-building operation is in Guatemala, but the Organization is also involved in peace-building activities in other countries, notably Sierra Leone, where it is monitoring human rights violations and helping the Government to implement its disarmament and demobilization tasks, and Liberia, where the United Nations has established its first peace-building support office.

67.   To ensure that the complex challenges of post-conflict peace-building are effectively addressed by the United Nations system and its partners, I designated the Department of Political Affairs, as convener of the Executive Committee on Peace and Security, to act as the United Nations focal point for this vital activity. I hope that the First Committee will soon rationalize its work along similar lines.

68.   A significant development over the past year has been the increase in civilian police operations, following the withdrawal of military personnel. Such operations have been conducted in Bosnia and Herzegovina, Croatia and Haiti and could prove very useful in other post-conflict situations, such as that in Angola. This development reflects a growing interest in the role that peacekeeping operations can play in helping to build human rights, law-enforcement and other institutions, and thus to strengthen the foundations of lasting peace.

69.   There has been growing recognition of the need to link all aspects of external support for countries afflicted

by conflict, whether political, humanitarian, developmental or human rights. The participation of donor Governments, host Governments and non-governmental organizations to meet this need is essential. The Administrative Committee on Coordination has been developing more coherent strategies for peace-building through the development of the new strategic framework concept. The framework defines the principles, goals and institutional arrangements needed to create a coherent, effective and integrated political strategy and assistance programme. It provides a common tool for identifying, analysing and prioritizing key issues and activities on the basis of shared principles and objectives. The framework embraces the entire range of core United Nations activities—political, human rights, humanitarian and development—in a given country.

Complementary strategies

70.   While the categories of prevention, peacemaking, peacekeeping and post-conflict peace-building remain useful, it is now widely recognized that most operations combine activities in more than one category. In some operations, for example, in Cyprus and Georgia, the United Nations is actively involved in both peacekeeping and peacemaking. In others, for example, in Sierra Leone and Tajikistan, planning for peace-building started during peacekeeping operations. These varied combinations are to be welcomed. They reflect an understanding of the complexities of particular situations and the need to coordinate a diverse range of security-enhancing activities.

71.   In the context of conflict prevention, the Department of Political Affairs plays a key role in early warning,

preventive diplomacy and peacemaking. Both peacekeeping and disarmament can contribute to conflict prevention. For organizational purposes, the work of the Department of Peacekeeping Operations is primarily logistical and operational, while that of the Department for Disarmament Affairs focuses on the diplomatic, legal and technical aspects of weapons and arms limitation. For example, the Department for Disarmament Affairs provides support for negotiations on international instruments to restrict or prohibit landmines; the Department of Peacekeeping Operations is in charge of action to deal with landmines in actual theatres of conflict. Both, however, have to operate within the framework of an overarching political strategy.

72. We now recognize more clearly than ever the crucial linkages between poverty, bad governance and abuse of human rights, on the one hand, and violent conflict on the other. To reduce threats to human security we must not only focus more on their underlying causes than we have in the past; we must also intensify cooperation among the various United Nations agencies and with the Member States.

2 Cooperating for development

73.   The challenge of development remains paramount in a world where one fifth of humanity is forced to fend for itself on a meagre dollar a day, one third of all Africans are not expected to survive past the age of 40, nearly 40 per cent of women in developing countries are illiterate, and more than half of South Asia's children remain underweight at age five, while the ongoing Asian economic crisis may thrust some 50 million people in Indonesia alone back into poverty. These stark realities persist despite the fact that the past half-century has witnessed one of the longest periods of economic expansion in history.

74.   Yet the volume of external aid to developing countries has declined steadily throughout this decade, and now stands at 0.22 per cent of the GDP of the industrialized countries—only 0.19 per cent for the group of seven major industrialized countries, which includes the richest among them. Moreover, donor countries are increasingly earmarking aid, with no guarantee that their aid-giving preferences match the needs of recipients. Foreign direct investment has not compensated for the decline in aid; in 1997 all of sub-Saharan Africa received a mere $3 billion, and South Asia $4 billion. Meanwhile, many developing countries, including some of the poorest, remain subject to the crushing burdens of external debt.

75.   The total development assistance made available by the United Nations is a relatively modest $5.5 billion per year. Despite its limited resources, however, the United Nations has unique advantages as a development institution. Its comprehensive mandate, spanning eco-

nomic, social and political domains, enables it to devise and enact intersectoral approaches to development cooperation; to link emergency assistance with longer-term development concerns; and to ensure that peace processes and efforts to achieve domestic political reconciliation are supported by and, in turn, complement progress towards development. In addition, the Organization's diverse institutional roles permit it to speak coherently across the entire spectrum of development cooperation, from normative to analytical, policy and operational activities.

76. My programme of reform begun over the course of the past year builds on this institutional capacity, and has already yielded practical results in the development area. The Executive Committee on Economic and Social Affairs was established early in 1997 to promote policy coherence in all economic, social and related activities of its member entities. Chaired by the Department of Economic and Social Affairs, it includes the relevant Secretariat units, the regional commissions, the United Nations University and the appropriate United Nations research institutes.

77. The Executive Committee has addressed a number of cross-cutting challenges. For example, it has drafted a proposal for utilizing the Development Account for consideration by Member States. It has initiated a long-term project to streamline the development indicators that are produced and used by the United Nations as well as by non-United Nations entities worldwide, and to ensure the consistency of their meaning and interpretation. The Committee also commissioned a review of all flagship reports in the social and economic sectors and has begun to work with the United Nations Development Group on the linkages between normative and operational activities in the field of development. Cooperation is also under way with the Office of the United Nations High Commissioner for

Human Rights and other United Nations entities to provide substantive content to the concept of the right to development.

78.   The United Nations Development Group, comprising the United Nations Development Programme (UNDP), the United Nations Children's Fund (UNICEF), the United Nations Population Fund (UNFPA), the World Food Programme (WFP) and other relevant operational entities, facilitates joint policy formulation and decision-making on development cooperation issues. New management tools are enhancing collaboration and the harmonization of procedures.

79.   Perhaps the most significant innovation at the country level has been the creation of the United Nations Development Assistance Frameworks. Developed jointly by United Nations country teams under the leadership of the United Nations Resident Coordinator and in close collaboration with Governments, they permit a new strategic approach to the implementation of goals agreed to at United Nations global conferences and of national development priorities, and make it possible to address in an integrated manner the many dimensions of poverty eradication. A year ago, the United Nations Development Group initiated a pilot phase to test the process in 18 countries; in two pilot countries the interface between the Development Assistance Framework and the World Bank's Country Assistance Strategy is being explored with the aim of fostering a strategic partnership between the two institutions. The pilot projects are now being evaluated and the lessons learned will inform future Development Assistance Framework processes.

80.   The Development Group has strengthened the Resident Coordinator system, which UNDP funds and manages. New selection procedures have been established that

are intended to increase the number of resident coordinators appointed from the wider United Nations system as well as the number of women serving in that capacity.

81. The designation of United Nations Houses at the country level—combining all United Nations programmes, funds and information centres in common premises—will contribute to a greater sense of community and common purpose among United Nations staff while also yielding increased efficiencies and, in many cases, reduction of costs. In 1997, United Nations Houses were officially designated in Lebanon, Lesotho, Malaysia and South Africa. It is expected that some 30 additional common premises will be designated as United Nations Houses in the near future.

82. Greater cooperation now exists between the Executive Committees on Peace and Security, Economic and Social Affairs and Humanitarian Affairs on issues including sustainable development, post-conflict peacebuilding, emergency relief operations, linkages between humanitarian assistance and development cooperation and the advancement of human rights.

83. These institutional innovations better serve the needs of Governments that count on the United Nations as a development partner.

Eradication of poverty

84. Guided by the outcomes of its major world conferences of the 1990s, especially the 1995 World Summit for Social Development, the United Nations has made the eradication of poverty a central cross-cutting goal of its activities. In May 1998, the Administrative Committee on Coordination, comprising the executive heads of all United

Nations entities, adopted a statement of commitment for action to eradicate poverty for the system as a whole. Its main purpose is to seek better coordination and greater cooperation between the various elements of the United Nations system, including the Bretton Woods institutions, and to agree on a shared strategy addressing all of the key dimensions of action against poverty.

85.   During the past year, the United Nations assisted some 100 countries with the preparation, formulation or implementation of national anti-poverty programmes. Reviews of existing strategies point to some key areas for improvement; there is, for example, the need to broaden the scope of action against poverty beyond the traditional social-sector and welfare approaches; to address such critical issues as access to productive assets; to encourage a more inclusive dialogue between the State, civil society and the private sector; and to target resource-poor communities and asset-poor households.

86.   A substantial share of UNDP resources—some 26 per cent of the total—is now devoted directly to poverty reduction. UNDP assistance includes support for poverty mapping, assessments of national capacity for poverty reduction, setting national goals and targets, public expenditure reviews, reviews of policies, administrative structures and procedures, and resource mobilization.

87.   In the belief that the eradication of poverty requires specifically targeting the social sector, the United Nations has given high priority to the implementation of the so-called 20/20 initiative, launched jointly in 1994 by UNDP, the United Nations Educational, Scientific and Cultural Organization (UNESCO), UNFPA, UNICEF and the World Health Organization (WHO). It was proposed under that initiative that Governments and external donors each allocate 20 per cent of their budgets to basic social services.

UNICEF and UNDP are providing increased support to reviews of country-level social sector expenditures.

88.   Achieving the eradication of poverty also requires that the feminization of poverty be reversed. Accordingly, the United Nations Development Fund for Women (UNIFEM) has supported pilot projects designed to strengthen women's economic performance. Efforts to increase women's access to credit, training and technologies so as to enhance their income-generating activities are also being supported. UNIFEM has played a pioneering promotional role in ensuring that the policies and programmes of microcredit institutions take gender issues into account. UNICEF programmes address the challenges of women's empowerment by enhancing the capacity of women's organizations and business associations to negotiate on economic issues, and by providing economic literacy materials to women.

89.   Poverty is a major cause of hunger, but hunger also causes and perpetuates inter-generational cycles of poverty. Relieving hunger is the first step in breaking those cycles. In 1997, WFP devoted 93 per cent of its development food assistance to the poorest communities and households in low-income food deficit countries, more than half of which was deployed in least developed countries. WFP projects seek to enable the hungry poor to reach a level of subsistence at which they can sustain themselves and thus participate effectively in mainstream development programmes.

90.   The World Food Programme has also carried out "vulnerability assessment mapping" in 22 African, 8 Asian and 2 Latin American countries. This exercise identifies the geographic distribution of poverty and food insecurity, and helps ascertain their underlying causes together with the appropriate programmatic responses. To ensure that the

poor have sustained access to food, WFP targets some 60 per cent of its development resources directly to women and involves them in the management of food distribution and in decision-making.

91.   Major steps have been taken to include respect for human rights and dignity as a core element in anti-poverty strategies, and to ensure participation by the poorest in their communities' decision-making processes. At its most recent session, the Commission on Human Rights appointed an independent expert to evaluate the relationship between the promotion and protection of human rights and extreme poverty. The Office of the United Nations High Commissioner for Human Rights strongly supports mandates that increase understanding within the United Nations system of the intrinsic linkage between development, democracy and human rights.

Social development

92.   In the area of social development, a broad array of normative and policy-level activities are under way. Preparations have begun for a review conference in the year 2000 to assess the implementation of the accords reached at the 1995 World Summit. UNDP has finalized a World Poverty Report, which documents progress towards the implementation of the Summit's goals, as well as the remaining obstacles.

93.   The General Assembly has designated 1999 the International Year of Older Persons; by this means, the Organization hopes to enhance the participation of older persons in their communities. In August 1998, at the other end of the generational spectrum, the third session of the World Youth Forum was convened by the United Nations in

partnership with the Portuguese National Youth Council at Braga, Portugal, and the World Conference of Ministers Responsible for Youth was hosted at Lisbon by the Government of Portugal in cooperation with the United Nations. The United Nations has also worked to promote the participation of disabled persons in society. Some 70 countries have now adopted legislation or established programmes to advance that end.

94. Health and mortality, and their relations to development, were the special theme of the thirty-first session of the Commission on Population and Development. The Commission called for more reliable and improved data on mortality, for action at national and international levels to determine the causes of the increased mortality noted among adults in some countries, and for increased efforts to lower mortality and improve health. Preparation is also under way for a special session of the General Assembly to follow up on the International Conference on Population and Development, which will be held from 30 June to 2 July 1999.

95. The lack of equality for women and violations of their human rights remain major impediments to development, democracy and peace. Preparations have begun for the high-level review to be conducted by the General Assembly in June 2000 of progress made in the implementation of the decisions of the Nairobi and Beijing World Conferences on Women. Concerted efforts are needed to attain the goal of universal ratification of the Convention on the Elimination of All Forms of Discrimination against Women by the year 2000 and to strengthen its enforcement mechanisms.

96. At the operational level, UNICEF and its partners help to focus worldwide attention on issues affecting children: the many millions who suffer from malaria and mal-

nutrition; the plight of those who serve in armies or work at hazardous or exploitative jobs; discrimination and violence against girls and young women; the nearly 600,000 adolescent girls and women who die needlessly each year from causes related to pregnancy and childbirth; the terrible toll that HIV/AIDS takes on young people; the many unmet needs of adolescents; and the widening gap between rich and poor.

97.   During the past year, UNICEF devoted increased attention to strengthening community involvement in matters concerning children and families. This has been the key to success in raising the number of girls enrolling and staying in school. UNICEF programmes have been expanded to reach not only infants and young children but also adolescents and youth.

98.   When reliable information is put in the hands of decision makers, supportive action on behalf of children and women becomes more likely and more effective. Accordingly, UNICEF has developed, in collaboration with several other United Nations agencies, a low-cost, fast and reliable household survey method, the multiple indicator cluster survey, a technique for building national capacity to track progress for children. These surveys have been carried out in 60 countries to date.

99.   In 1997, UNFPA devoted approximately 85 per cent of its total resources to basic social services, mostly aimed at the poorest and most vulnerable segments of the population. Essential activities included sexual and reproductive health education; improving adolescent reproductive health practices and tailoring them to specific country and subregional situations; providing assistance to reduce maternal mortality; providing emergency assistance in refugee situations; and supporting HIV/AIDS-prevention activities in some 132 countries. UNFPA funding also supported

population and development strategies and advocacy work. A set of indicators has been developed to help measure the progress, performance and impact of programmes in the Fund's core programme areas. This represents a significant first step in measuring the effectiveness of its activities.

100. Gender issues remained a cross-cutting concern of all UNFPA-supported programmes. Gender equality is also of concern to the United Nations Centre for Human Settlements (Habitat), which is promoting equitable access to housing, land and credit, and more broadly to the decision-making process in human settlements management. Through education and advocacy, UNIFEM contributes to strengthening the leadership skills of women in governmental and non-governmental arenas, and it trains women's organizations to monitor and promote the implementation of the Convention on the Elimination of All Forms of Discrimination against Women.

101. Within the United Nations Secretariat, the Organization is responding vigorously to its mandate to achieve gender equality. Progress has been made in increasing women's representation in the Professional ranks; at the senior levels (D-2), the proportion of women increased from 16 to 22 per cent. A more stringent system has been introduced to ensure that senior managers are held accountable for achieving the 50/50 gender distribution in the Professional categories mandated by the General Assembly.

102. The Joint United Nations Programme on HIV/AIDS (UNAIDS) seeks to build worldwide commitment and political support for the prevention and treatment of HIV/AIDS through advocacy based on technically sound and up-to-date analyses. UNAIDS issued its latest *Report on the Global HIV/AIDS Epidemic* this past June, just prior to the twelfth World AIDS Conference. UNAIDS also supports improved access to, and use of, the best and most effective

practices at the national and community levels. The Programme has made great strides in joint planning and programme coordination with other agencies and in forming partnerships with host countries as well as civil society actors. At the same time, paradoxically, explosive HIV growth continues in most regions of the world, and the prevention gap is widening between rich and poor countries. As a result, life expectancy rates at birth are declining in some developing countries to levels not seen since before the onset of industrialization, and gains in child survival rates are evaporating.

103. Fully two thirds of the people infected by HIV/AIDS worldwide are in sub-Saharan Africa. In addition to the tragic costs in human terms, the burden on already overstretched health and social facilities has been immense. The disproportionate impact on the young and on people still in their most productive years of employment adds to the direct economic costs and further diminishes the pool of talent available to societies.

104. In 1997, it was estimated that some 12 million people worldwide had already died of HIV-related causes; 30 million were living with HIV/AIDS; and 5.8 million were newly infected—some 16,000 new infections every day. These statistics were rendered all the more alarming by the fact that in many industrialized countries the perception prevailed that the "AIDS crisis" was over. Combination antiretrovirals have come into widespread use in the developed world over the past two years, but because they are so costly and difficult to administer they remain inaccessible to most people living with HIV in the developing world and in countries with economies in transition.

105. The examples of Thailand and Uganda show that HIV rates can be reduced significantly by strong prevention programmes. Uganda has cut its HIV infection rate by more

than a quarter, and Thailand by almost 15 per cent—reductions that compare favourably with those in industrialized countries. Stopping new infections is ultimately the best way of averting the devastating impact of HIV and success hinges on using a careful mix of tried-and-tested prevention methods. Some of these methods are extremely costly in terms of political capital, but they are essential if anti-poverty gains are not to be overwhelmed by this savage virus.

Sustainable development

106. The mutually supportive link between environmental protection and regeneration, on the one hand, and development and poverty eradication, on the other, has been stressed at least since the adoption of Agenda 21 at the 1992 United Nations Conference on Environment and Development. It was reaffirmed by the General Assembly in June 1997 at its special session devoted to appraising progress achieved since 1992. The Administrative Committee on Coordination is taking steps to translate agreed policy measures into activities of the United Nations system, especially at the country level.

107. Following up on the 1997 Kyoto Conference (third session of the Conference of the Parties to the United Nations Framework Convention on Climate Change), UNDP and the Global Environment Facility are supporting some 100 developing countries in the preparation of national situation reports. This $2.2 million project has already attracted $1.2 million in donor financing. It seeks to encourage the formulation of enabling legislation to respond to this major global challenge. It will also promote exchanges of information and knowledge among develop-

ing countries through South-South linkages. The initiative is the most recent in the UNDP $30-million-plus portfolio of climate change enabling activity projects. UNDP has published *Energy after Rio: Prospects and Challenges*, a report on the relationship between energy and development, which presents an analysis of the sustainable energy strategies that will be needed to meet Agenda 21 objectives.

108. Because half the world's population now lives in cities and towns—and an estimated two thirds will be urban in 2025—the sustainable development of our planet will more than ever depend on our understanding of urban problems and on the ability to craft and implement effective responses to them. The Habitat Agenda, adopted by the United Nations Conference on Human Settlements (Habitat II) in 1996, provides the strategic guidance for this effort. As recognized in the Agenda, success in meeting global environmental challenges depends on the effective management of urban problems.

109. The Sustainable Cities Programme, a joint effort of Habitat and the United Nations Environment Programme (UNEP), supports urban management at city and national levels through capacity-building and networking. The Programme is active in more than 20 cities and has produced a series of policy guidelines that are used in many countries. Habitat also provides the secretariat of the Urban Environment Forum, a global network of cities and international programmes committed to improving the urban environment.

Fostering investment and growth

110. A key challenge for the international community is to help the poorest developing countries, especially the

least developed, to build the capacities that enable them to become more effectively and beneficially integrated into the global economy. Debt relief, additional aid, better trade opportunities and more favourable terms of trade are required to facilitate this process.

111. The development of Africa remains a matter of the highest priority. I addressed the challenges of promoting durable peace and sustainable development in Africa in a major report to the Security Council in April. I urged the leaders of African countries that have been afflicted by cycles of conflict and lack of development to create a positive environment for investment by, among other measures, adopting the practices of good governance and instituting economic reforms. I urged the international community to do its part by converting into grants all remaining bilateral official debts for the poorest countries and to ease the conditions of access to multilateral facilities for the heavily indebted poor countries.

112. The growing marginalization of some countries in the world economy has been a major concern for the United Nations. Such countries typically exhibit high dependence on commodities. The declining importance of primary commodities in world trade appears to foreshadow a continuation of the long-term erosion in the prices of primary commodities relative to those of manufactured goods. Without success in diversifying their economies, therefore, these countries are likely to find their relative position continuing to worsen. The policy analyses conducted by the United Nations Conference on Trade and Development on such issues as commodity diversification, risk management and electronic commerce suggest new ways for small and medium-sized enterprises in developing countries to diversify their participation in international markets.

113. UNIFEM has been promoting women's participation in the trade and investment sectors. Studies on the
impact of trade liberalization on women workers were
undertaken this year in Africa, Asia and Latin America. In
addition, support was provided to women cash crop pro-
ducers to assist them in forming cooperatives to increase
their incomes and their bargaining position in the international economy.

Supporting good governance

114. Good governance is perhaps the single most
important factor in eradicating poverty and promoting
development. By good governance is meant creating well-
functioning and accountable institutions—political, judicial and administrative—that citizens regard as legitimate,
through which they participate in decisions that affect their
lives, and by which they are empowered. Good governance
also entails a respect for human rights and the rule of law
generally. Support for good governance has become an
increasingly important element in the development-related
work of the United Nations.

115. The support of UNDP for good governance focuses on strengthening parliaments, electoral bodies and
judiciaries. UNICEF provides support for the revision of
national laws in accordance with the Convention on the
Rights of the Child, training parliamentarians and law enforcement officials, and generally integrating children's
rights into the political and legal fabric of States.

116. Good governance is integral to the work of the
United Nations Office for Drug Control and Crime Prevention. A world free of drugs and drug lords cannot be
created without strengthening national judicial and law

enforcement systems. At the field level, the Office assists efforts to reduce demand for and production of illicit drugs, and provides technical assistance to law enforcement agencies in the fight against drug-trafficking. For example, the Caribbean Coordination Mechanism convened by the Office in Bridgetown, Barbados, explored ways to strengthen drug control cooperation in the Caribbean region, including maritime cooperation, harmonizing legislation and creating effective measures to counter money-laundering.

117. Supporting good governance, especially through strengthening national judicial systems and policy frameworks, is also essential to the promotion of reproductive health and gender equality. This past year, UNFPA provided assistance to Governments and sponsored workshops and advocacy efforts to further these aims.

118. The contribution of WFP to good governance focuses on capacity-building at the community level, aimed at enhancing the access of poor and crisis-affected households to food. The main means to this end is advocacy that the right to food be treated as a fundamental human right, the achievement of which is closely linked to women's empowerment.

119. The Department of Economic and Social Affairs has given priority to collecting and disseminating basic data on governance and public administration, so as to assist policy formulation and the development of long-term strategies in Member States. The Department has also fostered the exchange of information on practices and policies in the area of public sector reform.

120. Credible elections are a core ingredient of good governance and the process of democratization. Over the course of the past year, the United Nations continued to provide electoral assistance and to assist in strengthening

national institutions for better management of the electoral process. Since August 1997, the United Nations has received long- and short-term electoral assistance requests from Armenia, Cameroon, the Central African Republic, El Salvador, Equatorial Guinea, Guinea, Guyana, Honduras, Lesotho, Mauritius, Nicaragua, Swaziland, the former Yugoslav Republic of Macedonia and Togo. The United Nations also helped to coordinate and support international observation of the National Assembly elections held in Cambodia on 26 July 1998.

121. Meeting our commitment to enhancing economic and social development, particularly in countries in the greatest need, is an increasingly challenging task. Our agenda is expanding, yet our resources are declining. Effective cooperation among the various elements within the broad United Nations family of organizations is an imperative that we will pursue with determination. Achieving our goals will also require the strong support of Member States.

3 Meeting humanitarian commitments

122. During the past year, tangible results have been recorded in the humanitarian field despite serious funding constraints. Not only has the United Nations continued to provide humanitarian relief as well and as quickly as it could, it has also been the principal catalyst in finding more sophisticated ways of dealing with the plight of civilians in complex emergencies and in mobilizing the resources of the world community for this purpose as expeditiously as possible.

123. Unfortunately, there has been more evidence this past year of a further erosion in the respect for humanitarian principles in several countries. The right of civilians in need, particularly children and women, to receive humanitarian assistance is enshrined in international humanitarian law. Yet humanitarian organizations have been denied access to people in need and deliberate attacks on civilian populations have continued. Warring parties have terrorized populations into leaving specific areas. Hatred and suspicion between members of different ethnic or religious groups have been incited by media under the control of faction leaders. Increasingly, violence has been perpetrated against aid workers whose help to innocent victims of conflict is seen as threatening the political objectives of armed groups. The toll has been heavy: this year, for the first time, more United Nations civilian personnel have been killed than military personnel. I have asked for a report on what can be done to improve the security of our colleagues in the field, while still enabling them to carry on their vital missions.

124. The year has also been notable for life-threatening ecological disasters. The El Niño phenomenon, the forest fires in Brazil and Indonesia, a new drought in the Sudan, the tsunami in Papua New Guinea and other disasters have devastated thousands of lives. They have reminded the international community of the vulnerability of many parts of the world to both natural and human-created environmental disasters. The humanitarian consequences of such catastrophes are often so great that national Governments, acting on their own, cannot hope to cope with them.

125. In July 1998, the Economic and Social Council for the first time included a special humanitarian segment in its regular session, in which it reaffirmed the importance of respect for international humanitarian law and principles, endorsed the work of the Office for the Coordination of Humanitarian Affairs and set out specific goals for future priority areas.

Coordinating humanitarian action

126. The new Office for the Coordination of Humanitarian Affairs, headed by the Under-Secretary-General for Humanitarian Affairs and Emergency Relief Coordinator, focuses on three core functions: policy development and coordination; humanitarian advocacy; and coordination of humanitarian action. Operational functions have been transferred from the former Department of Humanitarian Affairs to other parts of the United Nations system. The newly established Executive Committee on Humanitarian Affairs, chaired by the Emergency Relief Coordinator, brings together relevant departments of the Secretariat (the Office for the Coordination of Humanitarian Affairs, the

Departments of Political Affairs and Peacekeeping Operations and the Office of the United Nations High Commissioner for Human Rights) and representatives of the United Nations humanitarian agencies on a monthly basis to address the humanitarian policy concerns of the United Nations.

127. The Inter-Agency Standing Committee, composed of all the key humanitarian agencies, has further strengthened its role as the primary mechanism for the coordination of humanitarian assistance activities. The Committee has established policy guidelines on issues such as the link between human rights and humanitarian action and the humanitarian consequences of economic sanctions. It also played an active role coordinating the initiatives of United Nations agencies and non-governmental organizations in support of internally displaced persons, including the establishment of a global database.

128. Policy development is one of the three core functions of the Office for the Coordination of Humanitarian Affairs. Humanitarian action can have important political, socio-economic and environmental repercussions. The Office has contributed to ongoing efforts to ensure a more coherent and integrated response to complex crises, for example through the "strategic framework" approach in Afghanistan. It has also elaborated clearly defined principles, based on the Charter, human rights and international humanitarian law, which would be applicable to all United Nations activities in crisis countries.

129. There are many opportunities for cooperation between humanitarian assistance and human rights programmes. For example, the wealth of information at the disposal of both humanitarian and human rights organizations can help to enhance the early-warning capacity of the United Nations, thus ensuring better identification of

needs for humanitarian and other assistance and allowing human rights programmes to be more responsive to country developments.

130. There is a widespread desire in the international community to counteract the harm economic sanctions impose on vulnerable segments of the civilian population in targeted countries. In a statement transmitted to the Security Council in February, the Inter-Agency Standing Committee expressed concern about the adverse humanitarian consequences of sanctions on civilian populations and urged that measures be taken to minimize them. The recent embargoes on Sierra Leone, and particularly the regional embargo imposed on Burundi by its neighbours, have curtailed the supply of foodstuffs and other *matériel* needed to alleviate the humanitarian consequences of those sanctions. Field evaluations of the potential and actual humanitarian impact of sanctions on Sierra Leone and the Sudan were undertaken in response to requests from the Security Council. In a study on more humane and effective sanctions management commissioned by the Office for the Coordination of Humanitarian Affairs, specific steps were recommended to address the humanitarian impact of sanctions and to facilitate the processing of humanitarian exemptions. The Inter-Agency Standing Committee has now set up a group of experts to develop the methodology further, and to increase the capacity of the United Nations to conduct impact assessment missions at short notice.

131. The Office for the Coordination of Humanitarian Affairs has continued to strengthen and integrate the collection, analysis and dissemination of information. The Humanitarian Early Warning System collects and analyses information from varied sources to identify potential crises, and it prepares briefs and reports on these. The Integrated

Regional Information Network, based in the field, provides information and analyses from a regional perspective to a variety of audiences in the international humanitarian community. The ReliefWeb Web site (www.reliefweb.int) consolidates and disseminates humanitarian information from over 170 sources, including United Nations agencies, international organizations, Governments, non-governmental organizations and other public sources. By the end of 1997, an average of 200,000 documents were being retrieved each month from ReliefWeb by users in more than 140 countries.

132. While progress was made in improving the United Nations inter-agency consolidated appeals process, of the total $2.05 billion sought as at mid-July 1998, only $472 million was pledged, received or carried over from 1997. Between September 1997 and August 1998, the Office for the Coordination of Humanitarian Affairs organized consolidated appeals for 10 complex emergency situations (Afghanistan, Angola, Democratic People's Republic of Korea, former Yugoslavia, Guinea-Bissau, Liberia, Sierra Leone, Somalia, Sudan and Tajikistan), as well as an appeal for the Great Lakes region and Central Africa covering Burundi, the Democratic Republic of the Congo, the Republic of the Congo, Rwanda, Uganda and the United Republic of Tanzania.

133. The number and scale of environmental emergencies have grown at an alarming speed. In South-East Asia, six countries were seriously affected by dense haze stemming primarily from large-scale forest fires in Indonesia. Fires also destroyed several thousands of square kilometres of forest in the Roraima State in Brazil, in March 1998. They were deliberately started for the purpose of land clearance, their spread being aggravated by El Niño–induced drought conditions.

134. In coordinating responses to 54 natural disasters and environmental emergencies from September 1997 to August 1998, the Office for the Coordination of Humanitarian Affairs issued 151 situation reports and launched 26 appeals for international assistance, towards which contributions worth over $129 million in cash, kind and services were provided by the international community. Ten missions were dispatched to disaster sites to assist with needs assessment and relief coordination.

135. New international and national arrangements must be put in place to ensure effective and ongoing coordinated support for disaster-reduction efforts in the next century. An action plan for 1998-1999 has been initiated by the International Decade for Natural Disaster Reduction secretariat under the auspices of the Office for the Coordination of Humanitarian Affairs to evaluate progress in disaster-reduction policies over the past 10 years, identify trends for the twenty-first century and shape future directions for international cooperation in disaster prevention.

Delivering humanitarian services

136. UNICEF has traditionally been dedicated to the provision of health, nutrition and education services to children and women in conflict. In 1998, efforts were stepped up to apply humanitarian principles to the impartial delivery of assistance to all children in need and to protect their basic rights. UNICEF worked with its partners to apply these principles in countries where access to humanitarian assistance is problematic, among them Afghanistan, eastern Congo, southern Sudan and Sierra Leone. UNICEF is also developing a training package in collaboration with the Department of Peacekeeping Opera-

tions regarding the responsibilities of peacekeepers towards civilian communities in general and the rights of children and women in particular.

137. Many of the World Food Programme's operations also come under the rubric of humanitarian assistance. The Programme's emergency work in 1997 focused on operations in conflict situations and reached a total of 19.1 million refugees or returnees and internally displaced persons, most of them women and children. WFP delivered food aid assistance both in life-threatening situations and for rehabilitation activities. Food aid assistance was provided to an additional 10 million people suffering the consequences of drought and floods in 1997. The Democratic People's Republic of Korea, a recipient of food aid during the year, has structural agricultural problems compounded by both floods and drought.

138. Natural disaster operations of a more traditional character were organized in 1997 in more than a dozen countries. Standby arrangements made in previous years with several non-governmental organizations and Governments were put to the test in 1997 in responding to the increased demand created by an abnormal number of natural disasters. Major contingency planning exercises were undertaken in 1997 for the Sahel region and southern Africa to prepare for possible droughts caused by El Niño.

139. Another source of serious concern during the year was the danger to the personal safety of WFP staff members, many of whom served in war-affected situations. Seven staff members lost their lives in the course of duty in 1997; seven more have died in 1998.

140. In addition to its mainstream development activities and resources, UNDP engages in special development activities designed to bridge humanitarian assistance with rehabilitation and recovery. These activities are funded by

5 per cent of UNDP core resources set aside for countries in special development situations. Since September 1997, UNDP has also participated in inter-agency efforts for United Nations mine action reform and policy development and has taken on the responsibility for addressing the socio-economic consequences of mines and unexploded ordnance.

141. In October 1997, I established the Office of the Iraq Programme to consolidate all Secretariat activities relating to the "oil-for-food" programme established pursuant to Security Council resolution 986 (1995). This is a temporary measure to provide for the humanitarian needs of the Iraqi people until fulfilment by Iraq of the relevant resolutions imposing sanctions. The Security Council authorized Iraq to export oil and utilize two thirds of the proceeds for the purchase of humanitarian supplies. The programme has made possible the purchase of foodstuffs, medical supplies and essential inputs for agriculture, water and sanitation, electricity and, recently, spare parts for the oil industry. In February 1998, I recommended a significant expansion of the programme and the Security Council subsequently authorized Iraq to increase oil sales up to $5.256 billion over six months, compared to $2 billion in each of the previous three phases. Because of a substantial drop in oil prices and limited export capacity, it is unlikely that sales will generate more than $3 billion during the current phase. There is therefore a need to ensure that food, medicine and spare parts essential to maintaining oil production receive the necessary resources.

Assisting refugees

142. The Office of the United Nations High Commissioner for Refugees (UNHCR) estimates that the total num-

ber of refugees, displaced and other war-affected persons fell by some 300,000 during 1997, to reach 22.3 million at the end of the year. This figure included 12 million refugees, 950,000 asylum-seekers, 3.5 million repatriated refugees in the early stages of their reintegration, and 5.9 million internally displaced persons and others, mostly from war-affected communities. A total of some 900,000 refugees were repatriated during 1997 either through UNHCR programmes or by their own means. Often, however, refugees returned to fragile or unstable situations emerging from conflict or still embroiled in it. In the former Yugoslavia, UNHCR remains preoccupied with the continued displacement of some 1.8 million persons, both within and outside the region. The conflict in Kosovo and the persistent tension in the Danube region of Croatia have necessitated a renewed UNHCR presence in the region to provide assistance to people fleeing those areas.

143. In western Africa, insecurity in Guinea-Bissau and Sierra Leone prompted outflows of refugees to neighbouring countries; Guinea now hosts one of the largest refugee populations in Africa. Post-conflict peace-building activities are being conducted in the region as Liberia begins the process of rehabilitation; between July 1997 and July 1998 UNHCR assisted almost 53,000 refugees to return to that country. In an effort to address the causes of refugee movements in the Great Lakes region and advance solutions, UNHCR and the Organization of African Unity convened a conference at Kampala in May, which focused on how refugees might be protected while taking into consideration the security concerns of particular Member States. The conference also addressed the complex and difficult relationship between humanitarian assistance and longer-term reconstruction and development.

144. In addressing the reintegration and rehabilitation needs of refugees and returnees, UNHCR faces an enormous task. Yet there is growing concern that its vital operations will have to be scaled down and, in some instances, suspended, because of lack of funding. This is especially so in the case of its operations in Angola, Rwanda and Liberia.

145. Combining both humanitarian and development work, the United Nations Relief and Works Agency for Palestine Refugees in the Near East continues to provide relief and social services to 3.5 million Palestine refugees in Jordan, Lebanon, the Syrian Arab Republic and the West Bank and Gaza Strip. With a deficit of $62 million in the 1998 budget of $314 million, which follows chronic budget shortfalls since 1993, the Agency's level and standard of service has however continued to decline.

146. The United Nations and its various relief agencies lead the international humanitarian efforts, often in the face of nearly insurmountable political and physical difficulties, as well as severe resource constraints. The key to alleviating the miseries stemming from man-made and natural disasters lies in linking those humanitarian efforts to the efforts being made in the political, economic and development spheres. Effective coordination between United Nations bodies and those outside the United Nations system is at the heart of this effort.

4 Engaging with globalization

147. Defined in purely geographic terms, little is new about globalization. Interconnected human activity on a worldwide scale has existed for centuries. The form of contemporary globalization is new, however. The production of a single automobile model, for example, or global trading in a financial instrument, may be physically dispersed across many countries. Yet those dispersed activities function as if they were all in one place, they are connected in real time and they follow their own holistic logic—whether it is determined by a single corporate structure or by thousands of individual buy and sell orders on computer screens and telephones. Moreover, demographic momentum, together with patterns of land use and energy consumption, has always affected local and subregional ecosystems. Today these and other human factors increasingly affect the planet's ecology as a whole, be it through ozone depletion, global warming or diminishing biodiversity. Lastly, the technological advances and open borders that enable commercial firms to organize the production of goods and services transnationally also enable terrorist networks, criminal syndicates, drug traffickers and money launderers to project their reach across the globe.

148. These new dimensions of globalization can only be addressed multilaterally, by the United Nations and by other international institutions.

The economic dimension

149. In cooperation with other multilateral organizations, the United Nations has sought to strengthen norma-

tive, legal and institutional frameworks that will allow the global economy to operate more effectively and equitably. These frameworks are essential to ensuring stability and predictability and allowing all regions of the world, in particular the least developed countries, to benefit from the expansion of the global economy. The international economic policy agenda today is beset with complex problems that were unimaginable when the rules for managing the post-war economic order were written in the late 1940s.

150. During the past year the Asian financial crisis has intensified and now affects countries on every continent. It has exacted steep and possibly long-lasting social costs in East Asia, and raised serious concerns about the operations of unregulated financial markets. Those hardest hit by the crisis are the most vulnerable; and there is a real risk that many of the successes built up over the years in reducing poverty in the region will be reversed.

151. As far back as 1993, the United Nations *World Economic Survey* expressed concern that a number of developing countries had become hosts to large stocks of volatile funds. The *Trade and Development Report, 1997* sounded a clear warning about the emerging situation in East Asia. Well before the onset of the crisis, the Economic and Social Commission for Asia and the Pacific (ESCAP) commissioned country studies to identify the strengths, weaknesses and remedial actions required to improve financial-sector management. Possible responses to the crisis have been discussed at meetings organized by ESCAP in cooperation with the Asian Development Bank, the International Monetary Fund and the World Bank; and by the Department of Economic and Social Affairs in cooperation with the regional commissions.

152. At a special high-level meeting on 18 April 1998 the Economic and Social Council addressed means of preventing or, if preventive strategies failed, of containing the impact of such crises, and of achieving "international economic security" more broadly. Questions addressed at the meeting included the overall health and viability of the international financial sector, the relationship between borrowers and lenders, and how to achieve the key objectives of poverty eradication and development. The positive atmosphere of the debate reflected the interest of the participants in moving towards a more comprehensive approach to crisis avoidance than currently exists, and in strengthening the cooperation between the United Nations and the Bretton Woods institutions.

153. Looking beyond the immediate crisis, the Economic and Social Council devoted its 1998 high-level segment to market access in the context of globalization, and debated how developments since the Uruguay Round are affecting developing and least developed countries. In a ministerial communiqué—a first for the Council—it stressed the need for further efforts for trade liberalization through the World Trade Organization, coupled with the need to provide enhanced technical assistance to developing countries. In September 1998, the General Assembly will, for the first time, hold a high-level dialogue on the social and economic impact of globalization and interdependence and their policy implications.

The environmental dimension

154. International cooperation has a vital role to play in arresting and reversing the potentially harmful effects of human activities on the environment. The Commission on

Sustainable Development and the newly strengthened United Nations Environment Programme are central to this effort.

155. The role of industry in creating sustainable development strategies has been of particular interest to the Commission this year. For the first time in a United Nations intergovernmental setting, the Commission convened a policy dialogue among Governments, the private sector, unions and civil society organizations on an equal footing. This led to an agreement to undertake a multi-stakeholder review of voluntary initiatives aimed at promoting environmentally and socially responsible business practices and investments. Such meetings will become a regular feature of the sessions of the Commission.

156. In June 1997, at its "Rio + 5" special session, the General Assembly had considered a study warning that, without preventive measures, two thirds of the world's population could face freshwater scarcity and water quality problems by the year 2025; in 1998, a series of international meetings sought to identify appropriate policy responses. On another front, the Commission's Intergovernmental Forum on Forests, at its first session in September 1997, adopted a three-year work programme, including consideration of a possible binding instrument for the sustainable development of forests and their resources.

157. A protocol to the United Nations Framework Convention on Climate Change was negotiated this past year. It specifies legally binding targets for greenhouse gas reduction by industrialized countries, and is a step towards managing major environmental problems attending globalization.

158. The United Nations also made significant headway in creating two new international legal instruments designed to ensure the safe management of hazardous

chemicals that move across borders. The first involves persistent organic pollutants that bioaccumulate, possibly causing cancer, reproductive disorders, damage to central and peripheral nervous systems and diseases of the immune system, and interfering with infant and child development. UNEP initiated negotiations to prepare an international legally binding instrument to reduce the risks arising from the release of 12 such pollutants. The first session of the negotiating committee was held in June-July 1998.

159. The second instrument concerns trade in hazardous chemicals and pesticides. After two years of negotiations, the draft text of a legally binding instrument prescribing prior informed consent of such trading was concluded in March 1998. This will provide a means to acquire and disseminate information on this risk-prone form of trade and promote shared responsibility between exporting and importing countries. A diplomatic conference is to be held at Rotterdam, the Netherlands, in September 1998 to adopt the convention.

160. In collaboration with more than 200 scientists and an international team of reviewers, the World Meteorological Organization and UNEP jointly prepared an updated scientific assessment of ozone depletion. That assessment notes that, with full implementation of the Montreal Protocol on Substances that Deplete the Ozone Layer, the complete recovery of the Earth's protective ozone layer could occur by the middle of the next century. It also indicates that the combined total of all ozone-depleting compounds in the troposphere peaked in 1994, and is now slowly declining. Like its predecessor survey in 1994, this assessment provides the scientific consensus needed to guide international cooperation for the purpose of phasing out the use of substances that deplete the ozone layer.

161. In the area of biodiversity, the Open-ended Ad Hoc Working Group on Biosafety held three sessions during the past year to continue preparing the groundwork for negotiations on a biosafety protocol to the Convention on Biological Diversity. The Global Environment Facility has agreed to fund a major pilot project to be implemented by UNEP that will provide assistance on biosafety to developing and transitional countries.

162. Regional multilateral organizations continue to play an important environmental role. For example, the negotiating committee on persistent organic pollutants agreed to use protocols established by the Economic Commission for Europe (ECE) as a basis for worldwide action. Similarly, within the framework of ECE, an international agreement has just been adopted to develop global technical standards for motor vehicles, which should lead to the production of vehicles meeting high safety and environmental standards.

"Uncivil" society

163. The globalization of electronic communication is helping to create an embryonic global civil society, represented most obviously by the ever-increasing number of non-governmental organizations focusing on issues related to the environment, development, human rights and peace. The forces that made possible the emergence of a global civil society also, unfortunately, facilitate the transnationalization of "uncivil" elements.

164. In many countries, criminal organizations and drug-trafficking syndicates with transnational links represent a major threat to both Governments and peoples. In June 1998, the General Assembly held a special session to

examine the global drug problem and related threats. It reached consensus that the most appropriate policy was a balanced approach to drug control, giving equal priority to reducing demand and reducing supply, and providing alternative crop opportunities to farmers growing drug-producing crops.

165. The operational follow-up to the special session will involve the key international financial institutions. It will also equip the United Nations International Drug Control Programme to assist countries in combating organized crime more effectively and in reducing the supply of illicit drugs. The Programme monitors and analyses changing drug traffic patterns, liaises with enforcement experts from other agencies and helps Governments to reinforce their border control and drug detection capacities. It has also developed a worldwide programme of training and technical assistance to increase awareness of money-laundering, encourage the adoption and enforcement of effective national laws and upgrade the skills of the police, prosecutors, judges and financial regulators and their ability to respond to the rapidly changing modalities of financial crime.

166. The Programme also maintains an Anti-Money-Laundering International Database; a world compendium of anti-money-laundering legislation and procedures, which is part of the International Money-Laundering Information Network; as well as a library and forum for information exchange among international organizations and other interested parties. UNDCP has also established a global system for sharing data with other international organizations involved in the fight against international crime. For example, its database is linked with Interpol and the World Customs Organization. At the regional level, the Programme brings together law enforcement authorities

from neighbouring countries to discuss region-specific problems and ways to address them. In drug-producing countries, it works with Governments and rural communities to facilitate a transition to legal alternative crops and promotes sustainable agro-industrial sectors.

167. The General Assembly took important action this past year to strike at the threat of terrorism. In December 1997, it adopted the International Convention for the Suppression of Terrorist Bombings. The Sixth Committee will next take up consideration of an international convention for the suppression of acts of nuclear terrorism.

168. In this increasingly interconnected world, the forces for good and evil travel with equal speed and ease. Globalization has an immense potential to improve people's lives, but it can disrupt—and destroy—them as well. Those who do not accept its pervasive, all-encompassing ways are often left behind. It is our task to prevent this, to ensure that globalization leads to progress, prosperity and security for all. I intend that the United Nations shall lead this effort.

5 Strengthening the international legal order

169. The idea that the international order should be based on legal norms and rules is fragile and fragmentary, but it is steadily gaining ground. A growing body of trade law, and other rule-based frameworks, allows global markets to expand. Multilateral treaties address problems related to the global commons as well as to arms limitation and disarmament. The United Nations plays a unique role in the definition and protection of human rights. Indeed, in 1998, the year which witnesses the fiftieth anniversary of the Universal Declaration of Human Rights, we are more than ever conscious of our responsibilities in this field.

170. It is fitting, therefore, that 1998 also saw the adoption of the Rome Statute of the International Criminal Court. The Rome Conference succeeded in creating what had long been described as the missing link in the international legal system: a permanent court to judge the crimes of gravest concern to the international community as a whole—genocide, crimes against humanity, war crimes and the crime of aggression.

The human rights regime

171. While gross violations of human rights remain an issue of concern, the notion that the interests of the many can be advanced by violating the rights of a few is an illusion which, happily, is far less widespread at the close of this century than it was in earlier periods. If individual rights are not protected, the whole of society suffers. Personal freedoms are however rendered largely meaningless

by civil wars, or by economic, social or cultural depriva-tion—often, indeed, by a combination of all these.

172. It is for these reasons that I have repeatedly stressed that the promotion of human rights must not be treated as something separate from the Organization's other activities. Rather, it is the common thread running through all of them, particularly through every stage of our work in peace and security, from conflict prevention to post-conflict peace-building and beyond. Human rights bodies are involved in early-warning and preventive activi-ties, and human rights considerations are increasingly em-bodied in our response to crises. We aim to provide human rights training for all participants in peacekeeping and humanitarian operations, and to put complementary hu-man rights field operations on a firmer financial basis. Building, or rebuilding, a national infrastructure for the protection of human rights is central to the whole concept of post-conflict peace-building. Finally, we aim to continue providing support for human rights institutions even after a country moves beyond the peace-building stage. The crucial connection between human rights and interna-tional peace and security is becoming more widely under-stood. Large-scale human rights violations are not merely the product of civil and ethnic conflict, they are also a major cause of such conflicts.

173. The year has also seen the United Nations begin to implement the rights-based approach to development, which is intended to help States and international agencies redirect their development thinking. The United Nations Development Programme has designated the right to devel-opment as a fundamental objective, and promotion of respect for human rights as central to development assist-ance. UNICEF has similarly employed the Convention on the Rights of the Child to guide its work.

174. The rights-based approach to development describes situations not simply in terms of human needs, or of developmental requirements, but in terms of society's obligation to respond to the inalienable rights of individuals. It empowers people to demand justice as a right, not as charity, and gives communities a moral basis from which to claim international assistance where needed.

175. On 26 June 1998 the international community observed the first United Nations International Day in Support of Victims of Torture. The United Nations Voluntary Fund for Victims of Torture channels humanitarian assistance to an increasing number of organizations that help victims of torture every year. Thanks to a substantial increase in the contributions received from Governments, the Fund will disburse more than $4 million in 1998-1999 for medical, psychological, social, financial and legal assistance to about 100 organizations that assist some 60,000 victims of torture worldwide. To further this vital work, I call upon those Member States that have not yet done so to ratify the Convention against Torture and Other Cruel, Inhuman or Degrading Treatment or Punishment.

The international tribunals

176. The two ad hoc international tribunals, the International Tribunal for the Former Yugoslavia in The Hague and the International Tribunal for Rwanda, have demonstrated that the institutions of international justice can have teeth.

177. Indeed, these judicial proceedings are of immense historical significance. The Tribunal for Rwanda is the first international tribunal to deal specifically with the crime of genocide. Its judgement in the trial of Jean-Paul

Akayesu and the sentencing of a former Prime Minister of Rwanda, Jean Kambanda, who had pleaded guilty, mark the first time ever that such decisions have been rendered for the crime of genocide by any international court. Without this Tribunal and the international cooperation it has been able to command, these and other individuals still awaiting trial—who all fled Rwanda—would almost certainly have escaped justice.

178. As at August 1998, public indictments had been issued by the two Tribunals against almost 100 people—60 by the International Tribunal for the Former Yugoslavia and 36 by the International Tribunal for Rwanda. In the case of the former Yugoslavia, 28 of the accused were in custody, five trials were under way and two defendants had been sentenced. In the case of Rwanda, 31 were in custody, including many of the alleged ringleaders of the Rwandan genocide, in addition to former Prime Minister Kambanda, five former ministers and other senior political and military figures.

179. To cope with the substantial increase in the workload of the Tribunals, and to prevent undue delay in the trial process, the capacity of both has been expanded, and elections will soon add new judges.

The International Criminal Court

180. On 17 July, after more than 50 years of hope interspersed with despair, and following five weeks of deliberations among representatives from 159 States, the Rome Statute was adopted by the United Nations Conference on the Establishment of an International Criminal Court. Its aim is to put an end to the global culture of impunity—the culture in which it has been easier to bring

someone to justice for killing one person than for killing 100,000. More than 200 non-governmental organizations took part in the process—an unprecedented level of participation by civil society in a law-making conference.

181. Although many would have preferred the Court to have been vested with more far-reaching powers, one should not minimize the breakthrough that was achieved. The Statute provides that States parties to the Statute accept the jurisdiction of the Court with respect to genocide, crimes against humanity, war crimes and the crime of aggression.

182. We have before us an opportunity to take a monumental step in the name of human rights and the rule of law. The main challenge now is to encourage States to ratify and implement the Statute. The Statute will stay open for signature until 31 December 2000. It is my fervent hope that by then a large majority of Member States will have signed and ratified it, so that the Court will have unquestioned authority and the widest possible jurisdiction.

183. The United Nations is an association of sovereign States, but the rights that it exists to protect and promote are people's rights. It follows that individuals everywhere have a responsibility to help defend the ideals of human rights. The role of civil society in the establishment of the International Criminal Court was an inspiring example of what can be achieved by people driven by faith in those ideals. The voice of the people brought us to Rome; the voice of the people gives this gift of hope to succeeding generations.

6 Managing change

184. The United Nations is a large, heterogeneous and highly complex organization. Managing its many activities and communicating its message are vital tasks. It is also in these areas that many of the most difficult reform efforts are being pursued. Success is absolutely essential if we are to meet our mission goals in the new millennium.

Creating a culture of communication

185. Placing communications at the heart of the strategic management of the Organization is central to the ongoing revitalization of the United Nations. If the goals of this revitalization are to be clearly understood, a culture of communication must pervade the entire Organization. Such a culture, supported by corresponding institutional arrangements, will enable the Organization to communicate with its global audience with greater coherence and forcefulness.

186. The Department of Public Information is leading the implementation of the new communications strategy proposed by a high-level task force that I appointed last year. The strategy focuses on enhancing the links between the United Nations, the media and broad sectors of civil society. Implementing this strategy will require us to seek out new ways to tell the United Nations story and highlight its successes. Towards that end, the Department and other Secretariat units are working together to identify and implement information campaigns, focused on news-making aspects of the Organization's activities. A strategic commu-

nications planning group has been created within the Department to assist the Under-Secretary-General in setting goals and strategies, and reaching out to the media, non-governmental organizations, academic institutions, the business community and youth.

187. The Internet has become a vital tool in strengthening United Nations partnerships around the world, given the primacy of speed in all media-related activity, and given also the access the Internet provides to vast new audiences. In future, the United Nations Web site will carry more audio and video material, including regular radio news updates; it will host on-line discussions with United Nations experts and promote the sales and marketing of United Nations publications and materials.

188. The United Nations Web site (www.un.org), winner of a number of specialist awards for its contents and ease of use, is being expanded to include all six official languages. During 1997, users accessed the Web site more than 40 million times; this number will more than double in 1998. A Web site created for the recent United Nations Conference on the Establishment of an International Criminal Court, held in Rome, provided instant news and visual material to the media and others closely following the issue. In its first two weeks, that Web site was accessed more than 380,000 times.

189. As part of the effort to deploy advanced communications and electronic publishing technology in all aspects of the Organization's work, United Nations Information Centres and services are now electronically linked both to Headquarters and to each other, providing instant, low-cost access to United Nations news, documents and reference resources. Several Centres have established their own Web sites for local audiences. On another front, the Centres are being integrated with UNDP field offices.

190. The print and audio-visual products of the Department of Public Information are increasingly tailored to meet the changing needs of media disseminators in terms of content, style and timeliness. This, too, has been helped by the introduction of radio and television programming on the United Nations Web site, as well as the rapid posting of digital photographs and print outputs of the Organization's activities worldwide. We are studying the possible creation of an international radio broadcasting service, which would put cost-effective information delivery at the disposal of the entire United Nations system, particularly in support of peacekeeping and humanitarian emergency operations.

191. Notwithstanding the vast opportunities offered by the Internet, the print medium is still the most influential in disseminating ideas and opinions. Department of Public Information publications are constantly reviewed and improved through readership surveys. Innovations include a more reader-friendly edition of *Basic Facts about the United Nations* and the transformation of the *UN Chronicle* into a lively forum of opinion and debate as well as of essential news. *Development Business* has launched *Development Business Online* in collaboration with the World Bank. Sales of United Nations publications continue to increase and are the leading revenue-producing activity of the Organization.

192. Outreach to young people is vital to the ongoing relevance of the United Nations. The Department of Public Information has placed special emphasis on education and youth, organizing guided tours, publications and workshops for teachers and students, plus special events such as Students' Day at the United Nations and a youth-oriented programme on Human Rights Day. The Cyber-SchoolBus, the Department's on-line education project,

reaches thousands of students in more than 60 countries, and is the most popular site on the United Nations Web site.

193. In the drive to build greater global public support for the Organization, the Department is working closely with non-governmental organizations. The Department is also expanding its contacts with research and academic institutions, the private sector, youth groups and global communication leaders. In September 1997, the annual Department of Public Information/NGO Conference, celebrating 50 years of partnership between the United Nations and non-governmental organizations, drew more than 1,800 participants from 61 countries to United Nations Headquarters. The second United Nations World Television Forum, held in November 1997, included a number of renowned television figures and provided a venue for a fruitful professional dialogue.

Administration and management

194. The Department of Management continues to focus on creating a mission-driven and results-oriented organization, which calls for better management of human resources and the Organization's programme.

195. The Department carried out a wide variety of initiatives last year. Programme managers conducted management reviews designed to enhance the delivery of mandated programmes, strengthen services to Member States and identify ways to implement their programmes within budgetary constraints.

196. In the future, greater emphasis will be given to what the Organization intends to accomplish in terms of results, as opposed to focusing on inputs and instrumental

measures. With results-based budgeting it is envisaged that the weak links of the programme planning, budgeting, monitoring and evaluation cycle will be strengthened. Evaluation studies will address the extent to which results have been achieved, thereby helping Member States to decide on the relevance and continuing value of programmes and subprogrammes.

197. The reduction of administrative costs and redeployment of resources will free financial resources for the Development Account, financing innovative activities in the economic and social fields. To this end, the administrative bureaucracy of the United Nations is being critically reviewed, with particular attention to simplifying and streamlining procedures; reducing administrative redundancies by delegating more responsibility to programme managers; creating a fully electronic United Nations; modernizing Secretariat functions; and discontinuing activities that have outlived their usefulness.

198. Close to 1,000 posts were eliminated in the 1998-1999 programme budget. Three departments were consolidated into one, while one department was re-established as an independent entity. In addition, I set up a human resources task force, which conducted an intensive review of the critical human resources issues facing the Organization. Its recommendations will improve the Organization's ability to evaluate its human resources needs more effectively, greatly accelerate the recruitment process, introduce better career planning and establish ongoing staff training programmes to ensure that staff skills respond to changing demands. Creating a results-oriented, high-performance Organization requires increased investment in human resources. Targeted learning and development programmes are being made available to staff at all levels throughout the Secretariat. Changes in the Performance

Appraisal System and other initiatives are indispensable elements in our efforts to introduce a results-based work culture.

199. Every permanent mission to the United Nations in New York is now connected to the United Nations via the Internet, and is thus able to access the United Nations Web site and all documents on the optical disk system. On-line virtual meetings are supplementing video conferencing, thereby reducing the need for travel and providing greater flexibility for meeting arrangements. Beginning-to-end electronic document management systems and other software are facilitating the transition towards a paperless office environment. These moves towards an electronic United Nations will be expanded in the future.

200. In solidifying and further advancing management reforms, the Department of Management will have to address a number of concerns. First and foremost is the need to ensure the full support and participation of all staff members in the reform initiatives. During the period of transition, the Department's primary challenge will be to guarantee that sufficient time and resources are invested in maintaining staff capacity, productivity and morale. Accordingly, adequate staff development opportunities and attractive conditions of service must be ensured. Continuing support by Member States for my management initiatives will greatly facilitate the Secretariat's efforts in this respect, as their support for flexibility, managerial initiative and responsive adjustments in the implementation of programmes will speed up the implementation of managerial reform and the delivery of mandated programmes.

201. The financial situation and outlook for the Organization during the past year have remained at best unchanged. As in previous years, projections for 1998 indicate that the Organization's combined cash reserves

will drop further, to about $577 million, from $669 million at the end of 1997, the regular budget portion again showing a sizeable deficit. While the level of unpaid assessments has remained relatively constant, a further deterioration in the pattern of payments has occurred because previously prompt payers are delaying their payments more and more. As a result, less cash is available and obligations exceed cash balances. With a decreasing level of peacekeeping activity, the future availability of peacekeeping cash to bail out the regular budget cash deficit is in increasing doubt. Thus, the Organization's cash position is weak and getting weaker.

Legal affairs

202. The Office of Legal Affairs continues to provide a unified central legal service to the Secretary-General, the Secretariat and the other principal organs of the United Nations and the Member States. Legal research services were provided to a number of bodies involved in the legislative process, in particular the two Commissions for which the Office serves as secretariat: the International Law Commission and the United Nations Commission on International Trade Law. Legal assistance was also provided for meetings of a large number of law-making bodies and conferences.

203. The Office of Legal Affairs participated in the drafting of a number of legal instruments, including the directive for the development of United Nations rules of engagement for military personnel and codes of conduct for staff members and other United Nations personnel. Advice was also provided on drafting a number of conventions and international instruments, including the Ottawa

Convention on Anti-Personnel Mines and the Kyoto Protocol to the United Nations Framework Convention on Climate Change.

204. The Office also advised States at the post-legislative stage, assisting them in implementing the provisions of the United Nations Convention on the Law of the Sea, and in the negotiating of additional international legal instruments compatible with that Convention.

205. Assistance was provided in the preparation and drafting of international agreements between the United Nations and other international organizations and institutions—for example, a relationship agreement with the Organization for the Prohibition of Chemical Weapons and a draft cooperation agreement with the provisional secretariat of the Preparatory Commission for the Comprehensive Nuclear-Test-Ban Treaty Organization. The Office also assisted in the conclusion of status-of-forces agreements between the United Nations and host States.

206. Another key activity of the Office of Legal Affairs was the negotiation of contracts, leases and other legal transactions of a private law nature which involve the Organization. The Office also played an essential role in devising major reforms in United Nations procurement procedures and developed a regime of limited liability in respect of third-party claims arising out of peacekeeping activities. The Office acted for the Organization in the settlement of claims brought either by the United Nations or against it, in particular commercial claims arising out of peacekeeping activities.

207. The Office of Legal Affairs represented the Organization before the two international tribunals. One case concerned the appearance of the former Force Commander of the United Nations Assistance Mission for Rwanda before the International Tribunal for Rwanda. An-

other involved requests made in the course of proceedings before the International Tribunal for the Former Yugoslavia for access to United Nations documentation.

208. Advice was provided to United Nations organs and bodies to assist them in discharging their roles in the resolution of international disputes. For example, legal assistance was given to the group of experts whom I asked to investigate the Scottish legal system in order to devise a solution to the continuing problems arising out of the Lockerbie tragedy. Non–United Nations bodies, such as the International Tribunal for the Law of the Sea, were also assisted.

209. Legal instruments were prepared to ensure that the activities of the Organization were carried out within their proper legal limits, an example being the elaboration of a draft Secretary-General's bulletin on fundamental principles and rules of international humanitarian law applicable to United Nations forces in situations of armed conflict.

210. The Office began implementing its redesigned information programme aimed at promoting understanding of the United Nations Convention on the Law of the Sea and thereby ensuring its consistent and effective application. Significant improvements were also made in the Office's publication programme. The production backlog of several regularly produced publications was eliminated, and new publications include an analytical guide to the work of the International Law Commission, a summary of the judgments and advisory opinions of the International Court of Justice and a complete index to the legal opinions appearing in the *United Nations Juridical Yearbook*. An audio-visual library in international law was established for lending to Governments and educational institutions.

211. In the year ahead, the Office of Legal Affairs intends to take advantage of the substantial recent increase in activity around the world aimed at reforming and modernizing commercial law by helping guide that activity in the direction of coordination, harmonization and unification of the laws of international trade. Yet another challenge of immediate concern to the Office will be to refine procedures and practices for coping, fairly and efficiently, with the increased number of requests for documents and other evidence expected to flow from the fast-growing workload of the two international tribunals.

Project services

212. The United Nations Office for Project Services provides implementation and management services to projects funded by United Nations organizations and programmes. Designed as an entirely self-financed and demand-driven organization, the Office functions like a business, yet in its operations it fully respects the values embodied in the Charter of the United Nations. It is now an important means for outsourcing inside the United Nations system. Demand for its services has been steadily increasing.

213. In 1997, the Office for Project Services delivered $463 million in services and goods worldwide and administered the disbursement of $151 million of loans by the International Fund for Agricultural Development (IFAD) to 63 countries. The Office has executed, or assisted in the national execution of, UNDP projects in all its focus areas. Contracted services span governance and poverty-alleviation programmes, environment programmes, and social rehabilitation and post-conflict reconstruction initia-

tives in 19 countries, including Afghanistan, Angola, Bosnia and Herzegovina, Cambodia, Haiti and Somalia.

214. In the framework of a 15-year-long partnership with the United Nations International Drug Control Programme, the Office for Project Services continues to participate in the implementation of a large portion of drug control programmes. New partnerships are being forged between the Office and other United Nations bodies, such as the Department of Political Affairs, the Office for the Coordination of Humanitarian Affairs, the Department of Peacekeeping Operations, the Office of the United Nations High Commissioner for Human Rights and the Office of the United Nations High Commissioner for Refugees. On behalf of the Department of Political Affairs, the Office set up mobile investigation teams and offices throughout Guatemala to enable the Clarification Commission to prepare a database on human rights violations, as agreed in the Guatemala Peace Agreements. The Office's Mine Action Unit is assisting in the design and management of mine-clearance programmes, notably in Croatia and Iraq.

215. For three consecutive years, the United Nations Office for Project Services has been able to operate successfully in accordance with the self-financing principle, generating enough income in implementation and supervision fees to cover all administrative expenses and to maintain a financial reserve at the prescribed level.

216. This performance is the result of the Office's own reform efforts. In addition to introducing value-for-money contracting, it has striven to lower costs and to improve the quality of its services by means of decentralization. Offices have been opened in Kuala Lumpur, Geneva and Copenhagen, as well as sub-offices in Nairobi and San Salvador. A new office was established in 1997 in Abidjan,

initially devoted to servicing rural development projects financed or co-financed under IFAD loans in western and central Africa.

Accountability and oversight

217. In its fourth year of existence, the Office of Internal Oversight Services has significantly contributed to my reform programme. Its activities have covered all offices, from New York and Geneva to Nairobi and Vienna, the regional commissions, and many separately administered funds and programmes.

218. Special emphasis was placed this past year on ways in which the United Nations monitors improvements in its operations and reform initiatives. In addition to auditing all peacekeeping operations, the Office of Internal Oversight Services reviewed the programme administration of the headquarters of the Office of the United Nations High Commissioner for Refugees and its field activities in 14 countries. The lessons learned from the liquidation and closure of peacekeeping missions in Haiti, Liberia and the former Yugoslavia have now been institutionalized, and UNHCR procedures for the selection and supervision of implementing partners—the Governments and non-governmental organizations that are responsible for roughly 40 per cent of UNHCR annual programme expenditures—have been made more effective.

219. Management audits have become a highly effective oversight mechanism. For example, a management audit of the personnel recruitment process of the Office of Human Resources Management showed that it was expensive and time-consuming (with the average recruitment taking an incredible 460 days to complete), but that the

Office was moving towards streamlining its practices. Similarly, a management audit of security at United Nations Headquarters found that this essential function was accorded a relatively low priority, and was neither adequately staffed nor funded. The Office of Internal Oversight Services recommended the allocation of additional capital funds to enhance the physical security of the United Nations premises, as well as a number of other security measures.

220. Guidelines on programme monitoring and evaluation were issued by the Office of Internal Oversight Services in November 1997, setting out the managerial elements of programme monitoring and evaluation that should be in place in each department and office. Training workshops and other services to help implement the guidelines are being established; the first workshop was held by ESCAP in December.

221. In-depth evaluations of the United Nations International Drug Control Programme and the Crime Prevention and Criminal Justice Division were completed. Reviews of the implementation of recommendations adopted by the General Assembly three years ago on the start-up phase of peacekeeping operations and on UNEP were also undertaken. The Committee for Programme and Coordination reviewed those reports, as well as a report on strengthening the role of evaluation in departments and offices of the United Nations, endorsing all their recommendations. The programme management evaluation of the Crime Prevention and Criminal Justice Division was also conducted. It was found that the programme has become less focused and priorities are not given sufficient attention. The Division immediately accepted the findings of the Office of Internal Oversight Services and its recommendations.

222. The Office also prepared my recent report on programme performance of the United Nations for the biennium 1996-1997, which reflects the extent of implementation of outputs identified in the programme budget. It indicates which programmed activities were modified during the biennium and which new activities were introduced, while highlighting the reasons for the non-implementation of programmed activities. Despite the financial constraints and the consequently high average personnel vacancy rate of 13 per cent, the balance sheet of the Organization in terms of output was largely positive: 80 per cent of mandated activities are implemented.

223. A follow-up review of the actions taken by the Department of Peacekeeping Operations in response to the recommendations made by the Office of Internal Oversight Services in a report to the General Assembly of August 1995 revealed that the Field Administration and Logistics Division had taken appropriate and corrective action to address the concerns raised by the Office.

224. In its drive to increase accountability, the Office has also played a valuable role in helping to bring to justice a number of cases of fraud perpetrated against the Organization. One case involved a senior staff member and a sum of some $600,000; others have involved outside contractors.

225. In the coming year, the Office will continue to support my efforts to reform and restructure the Secretariat in New York and major offices and programmes around the world. The focus will be on the restructuring of United Nations offices at Nairobi, as well as the reform of personnel recruitment and management, and the delivery of common services. A comprehensive review of the International Tribunal for the Former Yugoslavia will also be conducted.

226. In short, the critical institutional infrastructure that makes it possible for the United Nations to serve its clientele has undergone considerable change and innovation. Vital reforms in personnel policy must still be undertaken, but the Organization is more responsive, more efficient and more accountable than it was only a few short years ago.

.

7 Conclusion

227. One of the founding missions of the United Nations was to prevent the scourge of war between States. As we move towards the new century, the international community has largely realized that goal. However, while inter-State war has become a relatively rare aberration, threats to human security have by no means been eradicated. Savage civil wars persist, terrorism strikes at innocent victims and the AIDS epidemic provides daily proof that not only armies move across borders and kill people. In some parts of the developing world poverty seems endemic.

228. Recent experience has shown that the quest for international peace and security requires complementary action on two fronts: on the security front, where victory spells freedom from fear; and on the economic and social front, where victory spells freedom from want. Human security and equitable and sustainable development turn out to be two sides of the same coin.

229. This past year we learned more clearly than ever before that the forces of globalization profoundly shape our ability to pursue these objectives: that they pose extraordinary opportunities as well as enormous challenges. Globalization has generated an unprecedented surge in prosperity. The market-friendly development strategies that created the so-called Asian economic miracle, for example, delivered hundreds of millions of people from poverty in less than three decades. Those same market forces last year substantially overshot any needed market "correction". The consequences have been sobering—absolute declines in GDP, increased poverty, hunger, human rights abuses and violent social unrest.

230. Globalization puts a premium on good governance, and it can help devolve economic power from repressive regimes while creating the social space for the emergence of a thriving middle class and a robust civil society. On the other hand, it reduces the ability of Governments to deploy policy instruments free of external constraint and can thereby limit their capacity to help those most in need at home and abroad.

231. Global markets trade not only in economic goods but also in social ills—the illicit arms trade, for example, including components of weapons of mass destruction; the means to evade sanctions; the rapidly increasing traffic in human beings for sexual exploitation; the multitude of environmental challenges.

232. Globalization not only expands economic and social ties that unite; by corroding existing cultural identities it can also reinforce differences that divide.

233. The fact that globalization has these complex and potentially volatile consequences should occasion no surprise. Markets are purely instrumental means for the efficient allocation of resources. Maximizing the beneficial effects of market forces while minimizing their negative consequences has always required that they be coupled with the effective exercise of public authority: instituting the political and legal frameworks that markets require, and providing the safeguards against the deleterious effects they can produce. Whereas markets have become global, Governments remain local, however, and in key respects the capability gap between them is widening. Multilateral institutions have a critical role to play in bridging this gap. Only universal organizations like the United Nations have the scope and legitimacy to generate the principles, norms and rules that are essential if globalization is to benefit everyone.

234. The task ahead, therefore, is not to try to reverse globalization—an effort which, in any case, would be futile.

The task is to harness its positive potential while managing its adverse effects. Strengthening multilateral institutions can help accomplish that task.

235. If globalization involves costs as well as benefits, being on the periphery of the global economy is even more problematic. Nowhere is this fundamental reality more starkly confirmed than in the case of Africa. Vicious circles of unsound policies, predatory politics, natural disasters, violent conflict and the neglect of the developed countries have isolated large parts of the continent from the mainstream of global development. In my report to the Security Council in April, I addressed the sources of conflict and how to achieve peace and sustainable development in Africa, laying out a programme of action for Africa and the international community alike. In the past six months the situation, especially in central Africa, has visibly worsened. There have been too many false starts, too many pledges of uncorrupt rule routinely violated, too many broken promises of transitions to democracy. All of Africa's leaders must honour their mandates and serve their people, and the international community must do its part so that Africa can, at long last, succeed in the quest for peace and greater prosperity.

236. In the countdown to the new century, we must carry forward the reform programme I initiated last year, and Member States must engage those reforms that lie within their purview with greater determination and vigour. Reforming the United Nations institutional machinery is but a first step towards refashioning its roles for the new era. It is my hope that the Millennium Assembly will make this challenge its agenda. We all need a vital and effective United Nations—this indispensable instrument for achieving our common goals, this unique expression of our common humanity.

Index

(The numbers following the entries refer to paragraph numbers in the report.)

A

Accountability, 9, 101, 114, 217-226
Administrative Committee on Coordination, 8, 69, 84, 106
Afghanistan, 33
Africa, 34, 42, 48, 59, 61, 74, 90, 102, 111, 113, 235
Agenda 21, 106-107. *See also* Environment
AIDS, 96, 99, 102-105, 227
Akayesu, Jean-Paul, 177
Algeria, 39-40
Arms limitation, 11, 169
Arms trade. *See* Illicit arms transfers
Asia and the Pacific, 73, 150-151
Asian Development Bank, 151
Aziz, Tariq, 24

B

Beye, Alioune Blondin, 18
Biodiversity Convention, 161
Biological Weapons Convention, 22
Bretton Woods Institutions, 8, 84, 152
Business community, 10-11, 186

C

Capacity-building, 76, 109-110, 116
Caribbean Coordination Mechanism, 116
Central Africa, 42, 132, 216
Central Asia, 48
Charter of the United Nations, 1, 25, 30, 41, 128, 212
Chemical Weapons Convention, 22
Children, 12, 50, 73, 96-98, 102, 115, 123, 136, 158, 173. *See also* United Nations Children's Fund

Civil society, 3, 11, 16, 50, 85, 102, 155, 163, 180, 183, 186, 230. *See also* Governance; Nongovernmental organizations
Civilian police operations, 68
Climate, 12, 107, 157. *See also* Environment
Cold war, 1, 4
Commercial law, 218
Commission on Human Rights, 91
Commission on Population and Development, 94
Commission on Sustainable Development, 154-156
Committee on Economic, Social and Cultural Rights, 63
Committee on Programme and Coordination, 221
Committee on the Rights of the Child, 63
Commodities, 112
Communications, 163, 185-193
Comprehensive Nuclear Test-Ban Treaty, 21, 47-49
Conference of the Parties to the United Nations Framework Convention on Climate Change, 107
Conference on Disarmament, 47, 53
Conflict prevention, 24-27, 32, 41, 43, 54, 65, 70-71, 172
Conflict resolution, 39, 54
Convention against Torture and Other Cruel, Inhuman or Degrading Treatment or Punishment, 175
Convention for the Suppression of Terrorist Bombings, 167
Convention on Certain Conventional Weapons, 53

F

Family planning, 12
Food aid, 89-90, 137. *See also* World Food Programme
Foreign investment, 74, 155
Frechette, Louise, 6

G

Gaza, 145
Gender issues, 88, 100-101, 117. *See also* Women
General Assembly, 9, 12, 29, 45
  19th Special session to review and appraise the implementation of Agenda 21, 106, 156
  Special session on the drug problem, 164-165
  Special session to review implementation of the Fourth World Conference on Women, 95
Genocide, 35, 170, 176-177, 181
Girls, 96-97
Global Environment Facility, 107, 161
Globalization, 15, 147-168, 229-230, 232, 234-235
Governance, 72, 111, 114-121, 229-230. *See also* Civil society
Great Lakes Region (Africa), 18, 34, 132, 143. *See also* Rwanda
Greenhouse gases, 157. *See also* Environment

H

Habitat Agenda, 108
Haiti, 68, 213
Hazardous materials, 158-159
Health, 94, 103
Honduras, 120
Human development index, 15
Human resources management, 194, 197-198, 219, 222, 226
Human rights, 5, 11, 14, 27, 63-64, 66, 68-69, 72, 91, 114, 118, 127-129, 163, 169, 171-175

Human Rights Day, 192
Human settlements, 100, 108-109
Humanitarian assistance, 11, 122-146, 175

I

Illicit arms transfers, 50
Indonesia, 37, 73, 124, 133
Information dissemination, 119, 131, 159, 190-191
Integrated Regional Information Network, 131
Inter-Agency Standing Committee, 127, 130
Inter-American Convention against the Illicit Manufacturing of and Trafficking in Firearms, Ammunition, Explosives and Other Related Materials, 51
Intergovernmental Forum on Forests, 156
International Conference on Population and Development, 94
International Court of Justice, 210
International Criminal Court, 14, 20, 170, 180-183
International Criminal Police Organization (Interpol), 166
International Criminal Tribunal for Rwanda, 176-179, 207, 211
International Criminal Tribunal for the Former Yugoslavia, 176, 178-179, 207, 211, 225
International Decade for Natural Disaster Reduction, 135
International Fund for Agricultural Development (IFAD), 213, 216
International humanitarian law, 123, 125, 128, 209
International law, 169-183
International Law Commission, 202, 210
International Monetary Fund (IMF), 151
International Money-Laundering Information Network, 166

International trade, 110, 112, 153, 159, 233
International trade law, 169, 211
International Tribunal for the Law of the Sea, 208
International Year of Older Persons (1999), 93
Internet, 14, 131, 187-188, 191-192, 199
Iraq, 23-24, 141

J

Joint United Nations Programme on HIV/AIDS (UNAIDS), 102. *See also* AIDS

K

Kambanda, Jean, 177
Kyoto Protocol to the United Nations Framework Convention on Climate Change, 107, 157, 203

L

Landmines, 14, 19, 53, 71, 140
Latin America and the Caribbean, 42, 90, 113
Law of the Sea, 204, 208
Least developed countries, 89, 110, 149, 153
Lockerbie tragedy, 208

M

Mass media, 123, 186-188
Member States, 6, 9, 23, 29, 55, 59, 62, 72, 77, 119, 121, 143, 182-183, 195-196, 200, 202, 204, 236
Memorandum of Understanding (Iraq), 24
Middle East, 18, 38, 61
Millenium Assembly, 2-3, 16, 236
Money-laundering, 116, 147, 165-166
Montreal Protocol on Substances that Deplete the Ozone Layer, 160

N

Natural disasters, 27, 124, 133-134, 138, 146, 235
Non-governmental organizations, 11, 69, 127, 131, 138, 163, 180, 186, 193, 218
Nuclear Non-Proliferation Treaty, 21, 47-48
Nuclear terrorism, 167
Nuclear-weapon-free zones, 47-48
Nyerere, Mwalimu, 36

O

Office for the Coordination of Humanitarian Affairs, 125-126, 128, 131-132, 134-135, 214
Office of Internal Oversight Services, 217, 221-225
Office of Legal Affairs, 202-211
Office of the High Commissioner for Human Rights, 77, 91, 126
Office of the United Nations High Commissioner for Refugees (UNHCR), 142-144, 214, 218
Office of the Iraq Programme, 141
Oil-for-food programme (Iraq), 141
Older persons, 93
Open-ended Ad Hoc Working Group on Biodiversity, 161
Organisation for the Prohibition of Chemical Weapons, 205
Organization for Security and Co-operation in Europe, 41
Organization of African Unity, 41, 143
Organized crime, 147, 164-166

P

Peace, 17, 22, 25, 27, 45, 50, 68, 111, 163
Peace and security, 5, 17, 28-30, 39, 42, 47, 55, 172, 228
Peace-building, 28, 42, 69
Peacekeeping, 43, 56-61, 68, 70, 172, 190, 201, 206, 218
Peacemaking, 32, 38, 57, 70-71
Population, 108

Poverty eradication, 28, 79, 84-89, ⸱ 91, 105-106, 114, 152, 213, 227, 229
Preventive deployment, 43-44
Preventive diplomacy, 24, 31-32, 39, 41, 71
Public information, 185-193

R

Reform of the United Nations, 4, 9, 12, 45, 76, 184, 200, 217-218, 225, 236
Refugees, 99, 122, 137, 142-143. *See also* Displaced persons
Regional Centre for Peace and Disarmament in Asia and the Pacific, 42
Regional Commissions, 76, 151, 217
Register of Conventional Arms, 55
ReliefWeb web site, 131
Reproductive health, 12, 99, 117. *See also* Health
Resident Coordinators, 80
Rwanda, 177-178

S

Sahel region, 138
Sanctions, 23, 62-64, 127, 130, 231
Secretariat, 4, 6, 12, 76-77
    management, 6, 185-186, 194
    oversight, 217,219
    staff, 7, 101, 194, 197-198, 200, 219, 222
Secretary-General, 202
    Deputy, 6
    good offices, 18, 24, 31-32, 36
    reports, 111, 222, 235
Security Council, 29-30, 43-44, 56-57, 62, 111, 130, 141, 179
Social development, 5, 29, 54, 92-105, 121, 144
South Asia, 38, 74
South Pacific, 38
Southeast Asia, 48, 133
Southern African region, 138

Special Representative for the Great Lakes Region, 18
Standby arrangement system, 138
Status-of-Forces agreements, 205
Sudan, 18, 124, 130, 136
Sustainable Cities Programme, 109
Sustainable development, 50, 106-113, 155, 228

T

Technical assistance, 153, 165
Telecommunications, 163, 185-193
Terrorism, 147, 167, 227
The former Yugoslav Republic of Macedonia, 44
Torture, 175
Training programmes, 165, 172, 198, 220
Turner, Ted, 12
Twenty/Twenty (20/20) initiative, 87

U

UN Standing Advisory Committee on Security Questions in Central Africa, 42
UN system, 4, 8, 10, 67, 80, 84, 91, 93, 106, 121, 126, 146, 190, 212
UN web site, 187-188
UNAIDS. *See* Joint United Nations Programme on HIV/AIDS
Under-Secretary-General for Humanitarian Affairs, 126
United Nations, 2, 13, 16-17, 28, 31-32, 46
    agenda, 1, 121
    budget, 7, 9, 198, 201, 222
    cooperation with other organizations, 152
United Nations Assistance Mission for Rwanda, 207
United Nations Centre for Human Settlements (Habitat), 100, 109
United Nations Children's Fund (UNICEF), 78, 87-88, 96-98, 115, 136, 173